New wave mental maths

Eddy Krajcar and Lisa Tiivel

Prim-Ed Publishing
www.prim-ed.com

First Published in 2002 by Prim-Ed Publishing®
Revised in 2005 and 2012 by Prim-Ed Publishing®
Under licence to R.I.C. Publications®

© Eddy Krajcar 1999

ISBN 978-1-84654-496-5

Prim-Ed Publishing
sales@prim-ed.com
www.prim-ed.com

Copyright Notice
No part of this book may be reproduced in any form or by any means, electronic or mechanical, including photocopying or recording, or by any information retrieval system without written permission from the publisher.

FOREWORD

New Wave Mental Maths is a series of six pupil workbooks, written to provide a comprehensive and structured daily mental maths programme. The mental maths programme is designed to:

- *provide a structured daily mental maths programme for each academic year;*
- *encourage and develop mental calculation concepts and skills;*
- *develop and reinforce problem-solving strategies;*
- *develop and maintain speed of recall; and*
- *introduce, practise and understand a range of mathematics vocabulary.*

Assessment activities are provided for pupils to assess, monitor and record their own performance on a weekly basis. A separate teachers manual is available, to accompany the **New Wave Mental Maths** series. This manual contains: guidelines to help develop mental strategies; suggestions for classroom use; assessment; list of concepts developed and answers.

CONTENTS

Pupil record sheet	iv – v
Week 1	2–3
Week 2	4–5
Week 3	6–7
Week 4	8–9
Week 5	10–11
Week 6	12–13
Week 7	14–15
Week 8	16–17
Week 9	18–19
Week 10	20–21
Week 11	22–23
Week 12	24–25
Week 13	26–27
Week 14	28–29
Week 15	30–31
Week 16	32–33
Week 17	34–35
Week 18	36–37
Week 19	38–39
Week 20	40–41
Week 21	42–43
Week 22	44–45
Week 23	46–47
Week 24	48–49
Week 25	50–51
Week 26	52–53
Week 27	54–55
Week 28	56–57
Week 29	58–59
Week 30	60–61
Week 31	62–63
Week 32	64–65
Week 33	66–67
Week 34	68–69
Week 35	70–71
Week 36	72–73
Week 37	74–75
Week 38	76–77
Week 39	78–79
Week 40	80–81
Friday Test pages	82 – 101
Maths facts	102 – 108

PUPIL RECORD SHEET

Date	Week 1	Date	Week 2	Date	Week 3	Date	Week 4	Date	Week 5	Date	Week 6	Date	Week 7	Date	Week 8	Date	Week 9	Date	Week 10
	M		M		M		M		M		M		M		M		M		M
	Tu.		Tu.		Tu.		Tu.		Tu.		Tu.		Tu.		Tu.		Tu.		Tu.
	W		W		W		W		W		W		W		W		W		W
	Th.		Th.		Th.		Th.		Th.		Th.		Th.		Th.		Th.		Th.
	F		F		F		F		F		F		F		F		F		F

Date	Week 11	Date	Week 12	Date	Week 13	Date	Week 14	Date	Week 15	Date	Week 16	Date	Week 17	Date	Week 18	Date	Week 19	Date	Week 20
	M		M		M		M		M		M		M		M		M		M
	Tu.		Tu.		Tu.		Tu.		Tu.		Tu.		Tu.		Tu.		Tu.		Tu.
	W		W		W		W		W		W		W		W		W		W
	Th.		Th.		Th.		Th.		Th.		Th.		Th.		Th.		Th.		Th.
	F		F		F		F		F		F		F		F		F		F

New wave mental maths   www.prim-ed.com   Prim-Ed Publishing

PUPIL RECORD SHEET

Date	Week 21	Date	Week 22		Week 23		Week 24		Week 25		Week 26		Week 27		Week 28		Week 29		Week 30	
	M		M		M		M		M		M		M		M		M		M
	Tu.		Tu.		Tu.		Tu.		Tu.		Tu.		Tu.		Tu.		Tu.		Tu.
	W		W		W		W		W		W		W		W		W		W
	Th.		Th.		Th.		Th.		Th.		Th.		Th.		Th.		Th.		Th.
	F		F		F		F		F		F		F		F		F		F

Date	Week 31	Date	Week 32		Week 33		Week 34		Week 35		Week 36		Week 37		Week 38		Week 39		Week 40	
	M		M		M		M		M		M		M		M		M		M
	Tu.		Tu.		Tu.		Tu.		Tu.		Tu.		Tu.		Tu.		Tu.		Tu.
	W		W		W		W		W		W		W		W		W		W
	Th.		Th.		Th.		Th.		Th.		Th.		Th.		Th.		Th.		Th.
	F		F		F		F		F		F		F		F		F		F

Prim-Ed Publishing   www.prim-ed.com   **New wave mental maths**

MONDAY

1. Time? _____ . _____ or _____ past 5.
2. 2, 4, 6, 8, _____
3. 2 + 2 + 2 =
4. Draw a circle in the box.
5. Share 4 flowers between 2 people. _____ flowers each
6. 10 − 2 − 2 =
7. 7 + 3 =
8. 4 + 2 =
9. 5 + 5 =
10. 10 − 3 =
11. 9 − 2 =
12. Days in a year?
13. Days in a fortnight?
14. I am _____ cm tall.
15. Halve 10.
16. 1 m = _____ cm
17. Name this shape.
18. Double 4. 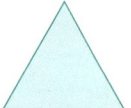
19. Is 9 odd or even?
20. 20 + 30 =

TUESDAY

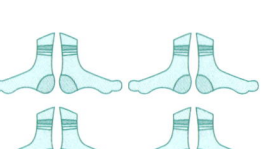

1. Time? _____ . _____ or _____ past 7.
2. 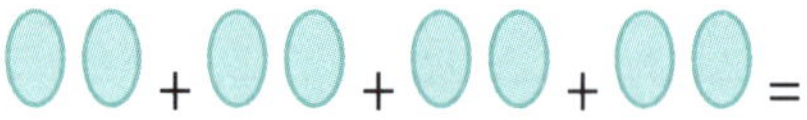 ⚪⚪ + ⚪⚪ + ⚪⚪ + ⚪⚪ =
3. 5, 10, 15, _____, 25
4.  △△ + △△ + △△ + △△ + △△ =
5. 8 − 2 − 2 − 2 =
6. Share 8 socks among 2 people. _____ socks each
7. Write eighty-six as a numeral.
8. 4 + 4 =
9. Share 5 apples among 5 people. _____ apple(s) each
10. 8 − 3 =
11. Tick which you would use to measure a pencil. ☐ cm ☐ m
12. 9 − 9 =
13. Days in a week?
14. _____ minutes = 1 hour
15. Name this shape.
16. Double 10. 
17. Halve 20.
18. Is 16 odd or even?
19. 2 m = _____ cm
20. 600 + 30 + 2 =

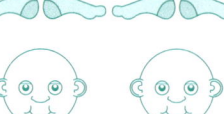

WEDNESDAY

1. Time? _____ . _____ or _____ past 2.
2. 10, _____, 30, 40, 50
3. 2 + 2 + 2 + 2 =
4. Write thirty-seven as a numeral.
5. Share 6 cakes among 2 people. 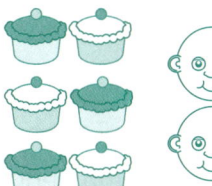
   _____ cakes each
6. 10 – 2 – 2 – 2 =
7. 10 + 6 =
8. Draw a square in the box.
9. 10 – 8 =
10. 7 – 4 =
11. Days in a year?
12. _____ hours = 1 day
13. Weeks in a fortnight?
14. 100 cm = _____ m
15. How many seasons in a year?
16. How many months in a year?
17. Name this shape. 
18. Double 3.
19. 40 + 30 =
20. 200 + 70 + 5 =

THURSDAY

1. Time? _____ . _____ or _____ past 10.
2.  ☐☐ + ☐☐ + ☐☐ + ☐☐ + ☐☐ = _____
3. 2, 4, 6, _____, 10, 12, 14
4. Draw a triangle in the box.
5. 12 – 2 – 2 – 2 =
6. Share 10 balls among 2 people. 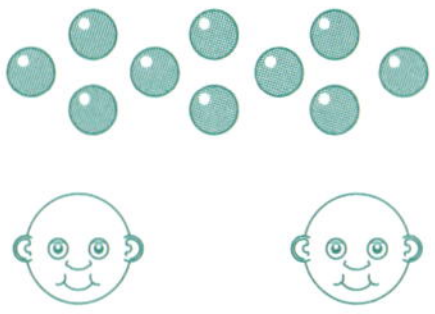
   _____ balls each
7. 3 + 3 =
8. 10 + 8 =
9. Tick which you would use to measure a garden. ☐ cm ☐ m
10. 0 + 4 =
11. 16 – 6 =
12. 7 – 5 =
13. Tick which you would use to measure a book. ☐ cm ☐ m
14. 4 + 3 =
15. _____ seconds = 1 minute.
16. Name this shape. 
17. Halve 18.
18. Double 5.
19. 700 + 60 + 3 =
20. 60 + 20 =

MONDAY

1. Time? _____ . _____ or _____ past 4.
2.  ☐☐☐☐☐ + ☐☐☐☐☐ = 
3. 5, 10, 15, _____ , 25
4. 6 + 3 =
5. Share 10 balls among 5 people. _____ balls each 
6. 15 – 5 – 5 =
7. Double 20.
8. Halve 60.
9. Is 15 odd or even?
10. A square has 4 equal sides. ☐ true ☐ false
11. Name this shape. 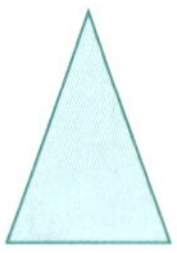
12. Tick which you would use to measure a chocolate bar. ☐ cm ☐ m
13. Measure this line. _____ cm 
14. Spring, Summer, _____ and Winter are the four seasons.
15. Days in a year?
16. Weeks in a year?
17. 27 – 10 =
18. Write one hundred and sixty-seven as a numeral.
19. 6 pairs of shoes = _____ shoes
20. 68 + 10 =

TUESDAY

1. Time? _____ . _____ or _____ past 8.
2. 5, 10, 15, 20, 25, _____
3.  ○○○○○ + ○○○○○ + ○○○○○ = 
4. 4 + 5 =
5. 20 – 5 – 5 =
6. Share 5 cakes among 5 people. _____ cake each  
7. 8 – 4 =
8. 24 – 10 =
9. Draw a rectangle in the box.
10. Is 22 odd or even?
11. Measure this line. _____ cm
12. Tick which you would use to measure a giant. ☐ cm ☐ m
13. Name this shape. 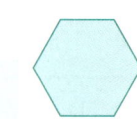
14. Name this shape.
15. Halve 22.
16. Double 7.
17. _____ seconds = one minute
18. Hours in a day?
19. 7 – 3 =
20. 100 cm = _____ m

WEDNESDAY

1. Time? _____ . _____ or _____ past 5.
2. 7 − 1 =
3. 97 − 10 =
4. You eat 2 eggs from a dozen. How many left?
5. ◯◯ + ◯◯ + ◯◯ + ◯◯ + ◯◯ =
6. 5, 10, _____ , 20, _____ , 30
7. Months in a year?
8. 10 − 5 − 5 =
9. Share 15 flowers among 5 people.
   _____ flowers each
10. 5 + 6 =
11. 3 + 7 =
12. Write one hundred and seventy-nine as a numeral.
13. Is 57 odd or even?
14. Draw an oval in the box.
15. Rectangle = _____ sides
16. What shape has 3 sides?
17. Double 6.
18. 38 + 10 =
19. Days in a fortnight?
20. _____ minutes = 1 hour

THURSDAY

1. Time? _____ . _____ or _____ past 11.
2. 10 + 27 =
3. Halve 20.
4. Is 15 odd or even?
5. Days in a leap year?
6. Days in a week?
7. 93 − 10 =
8. 24 − 10 =
9. △△△△△ + △△△△△ + △△△△△ + △△△△△ =
10. 5, _____ , 15, 20, _____ , 30
11. Share 10 socks among 5 people.
    _____ socks each
12. 25 − 5 − 5 − 5 =
13. Hexagon = _____ sides
14. What 2-D shape has 6 sides?
    (a) oval (b) hexagon (c) square
15. 2 + 9 =
16. You break 5 eggs out of a dozen. How many are left?
17. 1 m = _____ cm
18. 10 − 4 =
19. Measure this line.
    ├────────────┤ _____ cm
20. 300 + 50 + 2 =

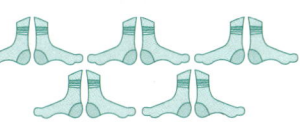

MONDAY

1. _____ past   `2:05`
2. In 561, does the 6 = 6 or 60?
3. In 73, is the place value of the 7 tens or units?
4. 50 − 10 − 10 =
5. 10, 20, 30, _____, 50
6. Share 10 sweets between 10 people. How many each?
7. 5 + 4 =
8. Write one hundred and forty-eight as a numeral.
9. 10 + 10 + 10 =
10. Is breakfast ☐ before ☐ after dinner?
11. What was last month?
12. 8 + 5 =
13. 25 − 5 =
14. Hexagon = _____ sides
15. Name this 2-D shape.
16. Measure this line. _____ cm
17. 300 + 300 =
18. _____ cm = 1 m
19. Take £5.00 from £11.00 = £
20. 9 − 5 =

TUESDAY

1. _____ past   `10:10`
2. 10 + 10 + 10 + 10 =
3. 3 + 2 =
4. 21 + 10 =
5. Draw a hexagon in the box.
6. In 179, does the meaning of 7 = 70 or 7?
7. 8 + 2 =
8. Is Friday ☐ before ☐ after Monday?
9. Share 20 cakes among 10 people. How many each?
10. 40 − 10 − 10 =
11. 50 + 20 =
12. What is next month?
13. 10, 20, 30, 40, _____, 60
14. Name this 3-D shape.
    tr_____ gul_____ pr_____m
15. 1 m = _____ cm
16. What day was yesterday?
17. Measure this line. _____ cm
18. Hexagon = _____ sides
19. 10 + 10 + 10 + 10 + 10 =
20. 400 − 100 =

New wave mental maths

WEDNESDAY

1. _____ past   [8:20]
2. Square = _____ sides
3. Halve 6.
4. 11 + 10 =
5. 94 – 10 =
6. In 89, what is the meaning of the 9?
   ☐ 900 ☐ 90 ☐ 9
7. 50 – 10 – 10 – 10 =
8. What year is this year?
9. 10 + 10 + 10 + 10 + 10 =
10. Draw a rectangle in the box.

11. 1, 3, 5, 7, 9, _____, 13, 15
12. 10 – 6 =
13. Share 50p among 10 people. How much each? _____ p
14. Name this 3-D shape. 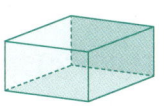
    c   b   i
15. Is March ☐ before ☐ after April?
16. What day is tomorrow?
17. 500 + 400 =
18. Double 15.
19. Halve 100.
20. 10, 20, _____, 40, 50, 60

THURSDAY

1. _____ past   [5:25]
2. 10, 20, 30, 40, _____, 60
3. 2 + 4 =
4. Share 30 flowers among 10 people. How many each?
5. In 34, what is the meaning of the 3?
   ☐ 300 ☐ 30 ☐ 3
6. Draw an oval in the box.

7. 5 + 7 =
8. 8 – 2 =
9. 91 – 10 =
10. Is Christmas ☐ before ☐ after Easter?
11. Write two hundred and seventy-eight as a numeral.
12. 500 – 200 =
13. Tick which you would use to measure a field. ☐ cm ☐ m
14. Name this 3-D shape. 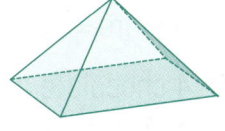
    p   r   m
15. What is this 2-D shape? 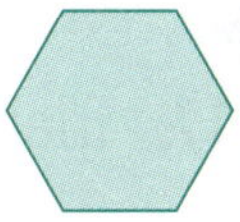
16. Triangle = _____ sides
17. 10 + 10 + 10 + 10 =
18. 80 – 10 – 10 =
19. Double 8.
20. In 540, what is the meaning of the 4?
    ☐ 400 ☐ 40 ☐ 4

MONDAY

1. _____ past _____ [5:10]
2. Round 17 (nearest ten).
3. 800 − 300 =
4.  ○○○ + ○○○ + ○○○ =  
5. In 635, what is the place value of the 6?
   ☐ 100s ☐ 10s ☐ units
6. What year was last year?

7. £4.00 − £2.00 =
8. Share 6 balls among 3 people. How many each?
9. 1, 3, 5, 7, ___
10. Name this 3-D shape. 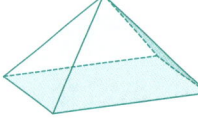
    p   r   m   d
11. 8 + 5 =
12. 80 + 20 =
13. Share 20 peaches among 5 hungry children. How many each?
14. 3, 6, ___, 12, 15
15. Square = ___ sides
16. 4 chocolate bars at 10p each = ___ p
17. Triangle = ___ corners
18. 12 − 3 − 3 =
19. What is this 2-D shape?

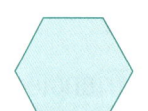

20. What day was yesterday?

TUESDAY

1. _____ past _____ [3:25]
2. 3, ___, 9, 12, 15
3. 7 + 1 =
4. Hexagon = ___ sides
5. 7 + 8 =
6. Round 76 to the nearest ten.
7.  ├─────────────┤
   How long? ___ cm
8. £1.00 − 50p =
9. ☐☐☐ + ☐☐☐ =
10. Share 12 cakes among 3 people. How many each?
11. 1, 3, 5, 7, ___, 11, 13, 15
12. 12 − 3 − 3 − 3 =
13. What year is next year?
14. 1 kg = ___ g
15. Rectangle = ___ corners
16. 2, 4, 6, 8, ___
17. Halve 30.
18. Double 13.
19. 12 − 7 =
20. In 526, what is the place value of the 5?
    ☐ 100s ☐ 10s ☐ units

WEDNESDAY

1. _____ past   [11:05]
2. △▽△ + △▽△ + △▽△ + △▽△ =
3. 15 – 3 – 3 =
4. Round 66 to the nearest ten.
5. 4 + 3 =
6. Share 15 sweets between 3 people. How many each?
7. 3, 6, 9, _____, 15
8. What day is tomorrow?
9. 2, 4, 6, 8, _____, 12
10. In 147, what is the place value of the 4?
    ☐ 100s ☐ 10s ☐ units
11. 1, _____, 5, 7, 9 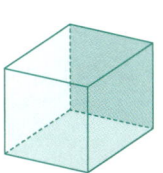
12. Name this 3-D shape.
    c_____be
13. What year is this year?
14. What month was last month?
15. 400 + 20 + 7 =
16. Triangle = _____ sides
17. 10 – 8 =
18. £1.00 – 40p =
19. Semicircle = _____ sides
20. 20, 18, 16, _____

THURSDAY

1. _____ past   [8:20]
2. 4, 8, 12, _____
3. £2.00 + £1.50 =
4. 6 + 6 =
5. 3, 6, 9, 12, _____, 18
6. Round 62 to the nearest ten.
7. 1, 3, _____, 7, 9, _____, 13, 15
8. In 294, what is the place value of the 2?
   ☐ 100s ☐ 10s ☐ units
9. Name this 3-D shape.
   tr_____ar p_____m 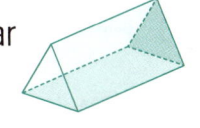
10. 200 + 400 =
11. 1 m = _____ cm 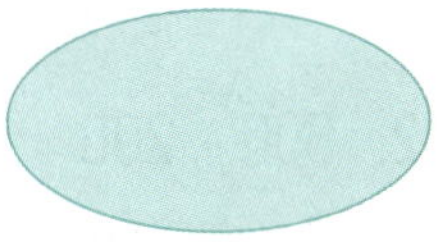
12. Name this 2-D shape.
13. Hexagon = _____ sides
14. 6 + 7 =
15. Share 9 apples between 3 people. How many each?
16. 18 – 3 – 3 =
17. 2, 4, _____, 8, _____, 12, 14, 16
18. 10 – 3 =
19.  ├─────┤ How long? _____ cm
20. What month is next month?

MONDAY

1. 5, 10, 15, 20, _____, 30
2. 4 + 4 + 4 =
3. 4, 8, 12, _____, 20
4. Share 8 apples between 4 people. How many each?
5. 12 – 4 – 4 =
6. Take £7.00 from £12.00.
7. Write two hundred and forty-seven as a numeral.
8. 36 – 10 =
9. 3 + 8 =
10.  How long? _____ cm
11. Tick which happened a long time ago.
    ☐ *You were 3.*   ☐ *You were 15.*
12. 600 + 200 =
13. How many blocks to fill the gaps? 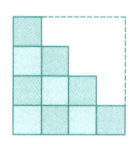
14. Double 9.
15. Tick which you would use to measure a playground.   ☐ cm ☐ m
16.  Vertical or horizontal?
17. Name this 2-D shape. 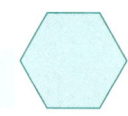
18. Which comes first?
    ☐ *Wednesday* ☐ *Friday*
19. 4, 8, 12, 16, _____
20. 800 + 60 + 2 =

TUESDAY

1. $\frac{1}{4}$ hour = _____ minutes
2. 4, _____, 12, 16, 20
3. Round 27 to the nearest ten.
4. 4 + 4 + 4 + 4 =
5. Buy 5 comics for £2.00 each.
   Cost = £
6. 3 + 5 =
7. _____ cm = 1 m
8. 2, 5, 8, 11   Rule = add _____
9. Name this 3-D shape.

   t   r

   p   m

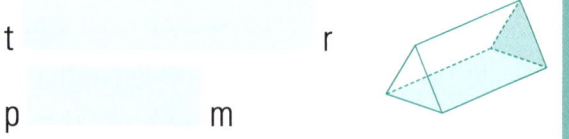

10. 5 + 9 =
11. A 2-D six-sided shape is a _____.
12. Share 12 books between 4 people. How many each?
13. £1.00 – 20p =
14. £5.00 – £3.50 =
15. 13 – 7 =
16. How many blocks to fill the gaps? 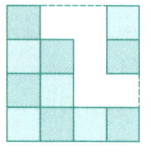
17. Half of 42 =
18. Tick which happened a long time ago.
    ☐ *You ate breakfast.*
    ☐ *Dinosaurs lived on earth.*
19. Which comes first?   ☐ *June* ☐ *April*
20. Vertical or horizontal?

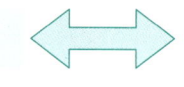

WEDNESDAY

1. $\frac{1}{2}$ hour = _____ minutes
2. 5 + 3 =
3. £10.00 + £4.50 =
4. 4 + 4 + 4 + 4 + 4 =
5. Which comes first?
   ☐ afternoon   ☐ morning
6. 16 – 4 – 4 =
7. Double 44.
8. Name this 2-D shape.

9. 4 + 9 =
10. 12 + 8 =
11. Hexagon = _____ sides
12. 30, 60, 90   Rule: add
13. Tick which you would use to measure your shoe. ☐ cm   ☐ m
14. Write three hundred and twenty-five as a numeral.
15. Vertical or horizontal?

16. 4, 8, 12, _____, 20
17. Name this 3-D shape.

    sp_____e
18. How many blocks to fill the gaps?
19. 39 – 10 =
20. 700 – 200 =

THURSDAY

1. $\frac{3}{4}$ hour = _____ minutes
2. Round 42 to the nearest ten.
3. 12 – 8 =
4. Write one hundred and sixty-eight as a numeral.
5. Share 16 bananas between 4 monkeys. How many each?
6. £1.00 – 70p =
7. 4 + 4 + 4 + 4 + 4 + 4 =
8. £10.00 – £5.50 =
9. 6 + 4 =
10. 4, 8, _____, 16, 20
11. 300 + 90 + 4 =
12. 6 + 8 =
13. Tick which happened a long time ago.
    ☐ You were a baby.
    ☐ You were an adult.
14. Which comes first?
    ☐ autumn   ☐ spring
15. In 389, what is the meaning of the 8?
    ☐ 800   ☐ 80   ☐ 8
16. 1 m = _____ cm
17. 4, 7, 10, 13   Rule: add
18. Hexagon = _____ corners
19. Is a square a 2-D shape?
20. 20 – 4 – 4 =

MONDAY

1. 1 hour =   minutes
2.   + 7 = 10
3. £5.00 +   = £9.00
4. Share 12 sweets between 4 people. How many each?
5. ☐ Clockwise or ☐ anticlockwise? 
6. ■■ + ■■ + ■■ =
7. Round 94 to the nearest ten.
8. Which comes first? ☐ September ☐ March
9. What day was yesterday?
10. 10, 20,   , 40, 50
11. Share £15.00 among 3 children.

    £   each
12. 60, 55, 50, 45,
13. Would you buy flour by the kilogram (kg) or the kilometre (km)?
14. Double 14.
15. 21, 23, 25, 27   Rule: add
16. 17 − 9 =
17. 12 − 6 =
18. Rectangle =   sides
19. Name this 3-D shape. 
20. Square =   corners

TUESDAY

1. $\frac{1}{2}$ hour =   minutes
2. Share 40 flowers between 10 people. How many each?
3. 6 +   = 9
4. Round 12 to the nearest ten.
5. 3 + 3 + 3 + 3 =
6. 16 wheels. How many cars?
7.   + 9 = 11
8. Name this 3-D shape.

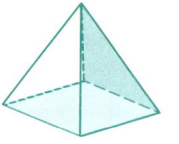

    s

    p
9. Hexagon =   sides
10. 4, 8,   , 16, 20
11. Measure this line.   cm 
12. Which comes first? ☐ breakfast ☐ dinner
13. 8 + 9 =
14. 10 − 3 =
15. Horizontal or vertical? 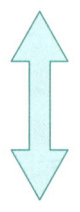
16. Write two hundred and thirty-two as a numeral.
17. 15 − 3 − 3 =
18. 3, 6, 9, 12,
19. 9, 7, 5, 3, 1   Rule: subtract
20. 5 + 5 =

WEDNESDAY

1. $\frac{1}{4}$ hour = _____ minutes
2. 4 + 4 + 4 =
3. What day is tomorrow?

4. 2, 4, 6, ___, 10, 12
5. Share 12 cakes between 2 people. How many each?
6. 5, 10, 15, ___, 25
7. £5.00 + £1.50 =
8. 500 + 200 =
9. Share 25p among 5 children.
   ___ p each
10. 16 – 4 – 4 =
11. Which comes first?
    ☐ Tuesday   ☐ Friday
12. 24 wheels. How many cars?
13. 2 + ___ = 8
14. Circle, semicircle or oval?

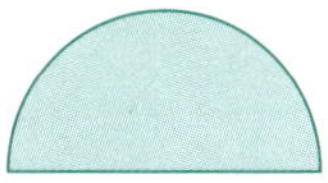

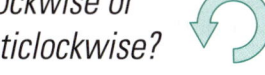

15. ☐ Clockwise or
    ☐ anticlockwise?
16. 10, 8, 6, 4, 2   Rule: Subtract
17. Triangle = ___ corners
18. In 258, what is the meaning of the 5?
    ☐ 500   ☐ 50   ☐ 5
19. Is this a hexagon?
    Y or N
20. 11, 9, 7, 5, 

THURSDAY

1. $\frac{3}{4}$ hour = _____ minutes
2. 15 – 9 =
3. £10.00 – £4.50 =
4. 3, 5, 7, 9,
5. 10 + ___ = 14
6. Name this 3-D shape.
   s 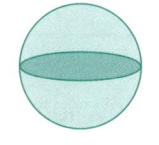
7. 5 + 5 + 5 + 5 =
8. 3, 6, 9, ___, 15
9. 32 wheels. How many cars?
10. 11, 13, ___, 17, 19
11. £1.00 – 90p =
12. Round 101 to the nearest ten.
13. £3.00 + £2.40 =
14. Which comes first?
    ☐ spring ☐ summer
15. In 209, what is the meaning of the 2?
    ☐ 200   ☐ 20   ☐ 2
16. 100 + 70 + 5 =
17. 20, 15, 10, 5   Rule: Subtract
18. 25 – 5 – 5 – 5 =
19. 10 + 10 + 10 =
20. Quadrilateral = ___ sides

New wave mental maths

MONDAY

1. Time?   . 

   ____ or ____ to 3.

2. Which comes first?
   ☐ Tuesday ☐ Friday

3. Horizontal or vertical?

4.  How long? ____ cm

5. Tick which you would use to measure a glove. ☐ cm ☐ m

6. What time does school start?

7. ☐ Clockwise or
   ☐ anticlockwise?

8. Round 46 to the nearest ten.

9. 3 + ____ = 10

10. In 478, what is the place value of the 7?
    ☐ 100s ☐ 10s ☐ units

11. 80 + 50 =

12. 12 + 6 =

13. What 2-D shape has 6 sides?

14. 9 − 2 =

15. 1 x 2 =

16. 10 ÷ 2 =

17. Halve 46.

18. 8 x 2 =

19. What is the number before 200?

20. 11, 15, 19, 23,

TUESDAY

1. Time?   . 

   ____ or ____ to 8.

2. Round 112 to the nearest 100.

3. ☐ Clockwise or
   ☐ anticlockwise?

4. Cube = ____ faces

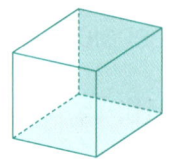

5. 4 + 7 =

6. 11 + 10 =

7. 17 − 5 =

8. Tick which you would use to measure the school hall. ☐ cm ☐ m

9. 6 x 2 =

10. Horizontal or vertical?

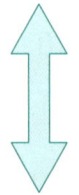

11.  Name this 3-D shape.
    c

12. 5 + ____ = 9

13. Share £40.00 among 4 people.
    £____ each

14. 700 + 200 =

15. 12, 17, 22, 27,

16. £4.00 + £6.20 =

17. 4 ÷ 2 =

18. 900 − 600 =

19. 2 x 2 =

20. Buy 8 pens for £2.00 each.
    Cost = £____

WEDNESDAY

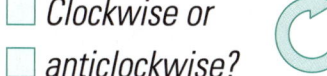

1. Time? _____ .
   _____ or _____ to 5. 
2. In a 50-m pool you swam 100 m. How many laps?
3. 8 + 7 =
4. 19 – 10 =
5. 21 – 9 =
6. Which comes first?
   ☐ autumn   ☐ summer
7. 10 + 10 =
8. 8 + _____ = 12
9. Write one hundred and seventy as a numeral.
10. Round 195 to the nearest 100.
11. 6 ÷ 2 =
12. 20 ÷ 2 = 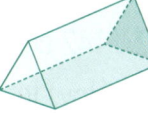
13. Name this 3-D shape.
    t _____
    p _____
14. ☐ Clockwise or
    ☐ anticlockwise?
15. 3 x 2 =
16. 7 x 2 =
17. £3.00 – £1.50 =
18. Name this 2-D shape. 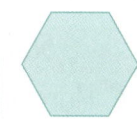
19. What time does school finish?
20. Cylinder = _____ surfaces

THURSDAY

1. Time? _____ .
   _____ or _____ to 3.
2. 8 ÷ 2 =
3. In a 50-m pool you swam 250 m. How many laps?
4. 16 ÷ 2 =
5. What 2-D shape has six sides?
6. Cone = _____ surfaces 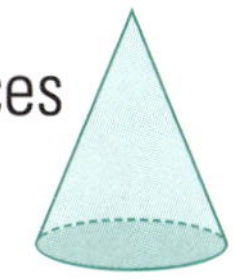
7. 14 ÷ 2 =
8. Tick which you would use to measure a pen.   ☐ cm   ☐ m
9. Name this 3-D shape. 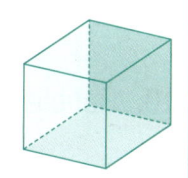
10. ☐ Clockwise or
    ☐ anticlockwise? 
11. 100 + 70 + 3 =
12. 20 + 30 =
13. 11 – 4 =
14. 15 – 6 =
15. £10.00 – £3.50 =
16. 7 + _____ = 14
17. Which comes first?
    ☐ November   ☐ April
18. Round 193 to the nearest 100.
19. 10 x 2 =
20. 4 x 2 =

MONDAY

1. Time? _____ .
   _____ or _____ to 4.
2. 12 − 5 =
3. 1 × 5 =
4. Name this 3-D shape. 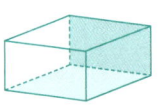
   c_____   o_____   d_____
5. What time does break start?
6. 15 ÷ 5 =
7. Treble 2 =
8. 125 cm = _____ m _____ cm
9. Which comes first?
   ☐ Monday   ☐ Friday
10. Double 5 =
11. 9 × 5 =
12. 35 ÷ 5 =
13. 4 + 8 =
14. 28 + 10 =
15. 10 + _____ = 15
16. 25, 45, 65, _____
17. Rectangle = _____ sides
18. Rectangle = _____ corners
19. Round 143 to the nearest ten.
20. Tick the pyramid.

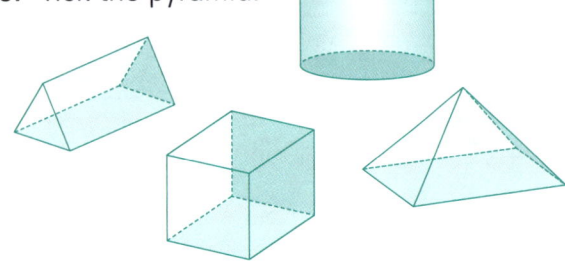

TUESDAY

1. Time? _____ .
   _____ or _____ to 11.
2. Share 12 pieces of chocolate among 6 smiling children.
   _____ pieces each
3. 2 × 5 =
4. 14 − 5 =
5. 19 − 10 =
6. 8 × 5 =
7. 10, 12, _____, 16, 18, 20
8. 10 ÷ 5 =
9. 900 − 300 =
10. 11 + _____ = 16
11. 40 + 80 =
12. 142 cm = _____ m _____ cm
13. How long? _____ cm
14. 10 × 5 =
15. Name this 2-D shape. 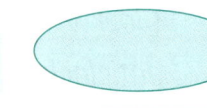
16. What time does break finish?
17. Which comes first?
    ☐ May   ☐ July
18. In 395, what is the meaning of the 5?
    ☐ 500   ☐ 50   ☐ 5
19. Horizontal or vertical? 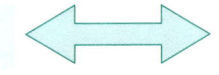
20. Hexagon = _____ sides

WEDNESDAY

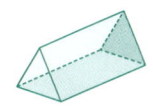

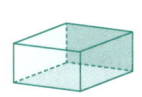

1. Time? _____ .
   or _____ to 2.
2. 20 ÷ 5 =
3. Would you ask for a kilogram or a kilometre of steak?
4. 200 + 600 =
5. Round 43 to the nearest ten.
6. Tick the triangular prism.
7. 154 cm = ____ m ____ cm
8. What time does lunch break start?
9. Is coffee sold by the gram or by the centimetre?
10. 12 – 4 =
11. Triangle = ____ sides
12. Name this 3-D shape.
    c
13. 12 + ____ = 18 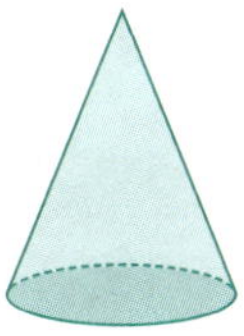
14. 3 x 5 =
15. Write two hundred and twenty-eight as numeral.
16. 6 + 7 =
17. 140 – 40 =
18. 11, 13, 15, ____ , 19
19. 19 – 4 =
20. 60 + 30 + 30 =

THURSDAY

1. Time? _____ .
   or _____ to 5.
2. 6 x 5 =
3. 5 ÷ 5 =
4. 31 + 10 =
5. Square pyramid = ____ faces 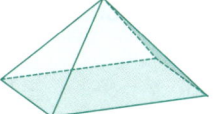
6. 25 ÷ 5 =
7. Name this 3-D shape
   c _____ d
8. 6 – 3 = 
9. 40 ÷ 5 =
10. Round 121 to the nearest ten.
11. 5 x 5 =
12. £12.00 – £2.50 =
13. Is milk sold in litres or metres?
14. Name this 2-D shape.
15. 9 + 6 = 
16. 50 + 70 =
17. Treble 5 =
18. ☐ Clockwise or
    ☐ anticlockwise?
19. What time does lunch break finish? 
20. Which comes first?
    ☐ Boxing Day   ☐ St George's Day

MONDAY

1. _____ to [8:35]
2. 1 x 10 =
3. Can a cone roll in a straight line?
4. What time does lunch break start?
5. 7 + _____ = 15
6. Name this 3-D shape.

    c
7. 235 cm = _____ m _____ cm
8. 5 + 8 =
9. 15 – 7 =
10. 400 + 500 =
11. 7 + 9 =
12. 10, 12, 14, 16, _____, 20
13. £8.30 + £5.00 =
14. 30 ÷ 10 =
15. 5, 10, 15, 20, _____
16. Which comes first?
    ☐ September ☐ October
17. Round 16 to the nearest ten.
18. Name this 2-D shape.

19. Hexagon = _____ sides
20. Write three hundred and forty-five as a numeral.

TUESDAY

1. _____ to [10:50]
2. 80 + 60 =
3. 3 x 10 =
4. 8 x 10 =
5. 91 – 10 =
6. 100, 98, 96, _____
7. Square = _____ sides
8. Name this 3-D shape.

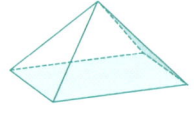

    p
9. Which comes first?
    ☐ Saturday ☐ Friday
10. What time does lunch break finish?
11. Would you weigh yourself in kilograms or kilometres?
12. 459 cm = _____ m _____ cm
13. In 794, what is the place value of the 9?
    ☐ 100s ☐ 10s ☐ units
14. Double 19.
15. 2 x 10 =
16. 40 ÷ 10 =
17. 900 – 400 =
18. 6 + 5 =
19. Name this 3-D shape.

    c
20. 3 + 5 + 4 =

WEDNESDAY

1. _____ to _____ | 2:40 |
2. 50 ÷ 10 =
3. 70 ÷ 10 =
4. Name this 2-D shape. 
5. Which comes first?
   ☐ autumn ☐ spring
6. 4 x 10 =
7. £10.00 – £1.50 =
8. 12 – 7 =
9. What time does school finish?
10. 921 cm = _____ m _____ cm
11. 12 + _____ = 20
12. Name this 2-D shape. 
13. 6 x 10 =
14. 8 + 9 =
15. £1.00 – 60p =
16. Share £36.00 among 4 teachers.
    £_____ each
17. Triangular prism = _____ faces 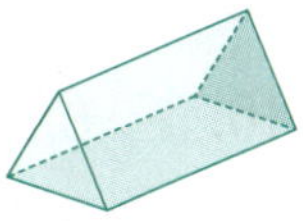
18. 40 + 90 =
19. 11 – 6 =
20. Cube = _____ corners

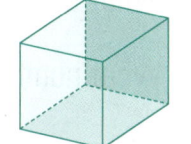

THURSDAY

1. _____ to _____ | 12:55 |
2. 5 x 10 =
3. 7 x 10 =
4. 20 ÷ 10 =
5. 4, 9, 14, 19, _____
6. 9 x 10 =
7. Name this 2-D shape. 
8. Round 17 to the nearest ten.
9. Do you buy bananas by the kilogram or the kilometre?
10. 6, 12, 18, _____
11. 11, 13, 15, _____, 19
12. Cone = _____ corners 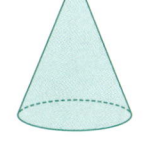
13. Vertical or horizontal? 
14. Name this 3-D shape. 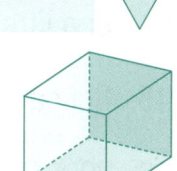
15. 14 + _____ = 19
16. 11 – 8 =
17. 13 – 4 =
18. Is paint sold in litres or metres?
19. What time does school start?
20. Which comes first?
    ☐ evening ☐ morning

MONDAY

1. _____ to [3:40]
2. 2 x 2 =
3. 7 + 4 =
4. 7 + 5 =
5. Name this 2-D shape.

6. Horizontal or vertical?

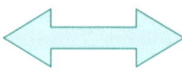

7. Name this 2-D shape.

8. 8 + ___ = 14
9. 9 x 5 =
10. 300 + 200 =
11. 40 – 10 =
12. 3 x 10 =
13. 365 cm = ___ m ___ cm
14. Would you drink a metre or a litre of milk?
15. Round 143 to the nearest ten.
16. 20 ÷ 2 =
17. 30 ÷ 5 =
18. 8 x 10 =
19. If a baby uses 5 nappies in a day, how many will be used in one week?

20. 3, 8, 13, 18, ___   Rule: add

TUESDAY

1. _____ to [5:55]
2. 4 x 2 =
3. 7 x 5 =
4. Name this 3-D shape.

5. 5 x 10 =
6. Would you eat a kilometre or kilogram of grapes?

7. Round 115 to the nearest ten.

8. 18 ÷ 2 =
9. 20 ÷ 5 =
10. 15 – 9 =
11. 14 – 7 =
12. 3, 7, 12, 18, ___
13. Name this 3-D shape.

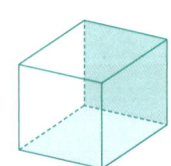

14. £5.50 – £5.00 =
15. Hexagon = ___ sides
16. ☐ Clockwise or ☐ anticlockwise?
17. What time does school finish?
18. What number comes after 49?
19. 563 cm = ___ m ___ cm
20. 80 + 30 =

WEDNESDAY

[10:50]

1. _____ to _____
2. 5 x 5 =
3. 6 x 2 =
4. 10 x 10 =
5. 16 – 9 =
6. 13 – 9 =
7. Hexagon = _____ corners
8. Triangle = _____ sides
9. 8 + 6 =
10. What time does lunch break finish?
11. 500 + 400 =
12. Round 129 to the nearest ten.
13. 18, 17, 16, 15   Rule: Subtract
14. 16 ÷ 2 =
15. £10.00 – £8.50 =
16. Is this an oval? 
17. 12 + _____ = 19
18. What time does school start?
19. 742 cm = _____ m _____ cm
20. Seven cyclists need new tyres for their bikes. How many tyres are needed?

THURSDAY

[11:35]

1. _____ to _____
2. 14 ÷ 2 =
3. 80 ÷ 10 =
4. 100 + 85 =
5. 2 + 9 =
6. Name this 3-D shape. 
   _____ e
7. What time does lunch break start?
8. 962 cm = _____ m _____ cm
9. Round 72 to the nearest ten.
10. Is this a sphere? 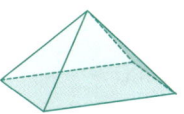
11. 12 – 6 =
12. 10 ÷ 5 =
13. 8 x 2 =
14. 3 x 5 =
15. 7 x 10 =
16. Triangular prism = _____ corners 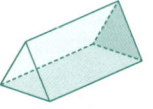
17. 2 x 10 =
18. 3, 6, 9, 12, _____ 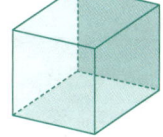
19. Cube = _____ faces
20. 14 + _____ = 22

New wave mental maths

MONDAY

1. _____ to [2:35]
2. 4 fish in a tank, add 9 more.

    _____ fish

3. 3 + 5 =
4. 4 x 3 =
5. Name this 3-D shape.

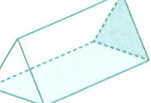

    t

    p   m

6. 70 minutes = _____ hour(s)

    _____ minute(s)

7. Draw a line of symmetry.
8. Halve 50.
9. Tick which shape will roll.
10. 4 + 4 + 4 + 4 =
11. 8 x 3 =
12. Name this 2-D shape.

13. £1.25 = _____ p
14. 1 L = _____ mL
15. Round 33 to the nearest 10.
16. If the date is 15.5.05, what is the month?

17. 6 ÷ 3 =
18. 12 – 7 =
19. What comes next?

    ○ □ △ ○ □

20. 70 + 30 =

TUESDAY

1. _____ to [10:55]
2. 18 – 9 =
3. |———————|

    Measure this line. _____ cm

4. 16 km + 7 km = _____ km
5. If the date is 14.6.05, what is the month?
6. Double 15.
7. 14 – 9 =
8. Draw a line of symmetry.
9. Name this 2-D shape.

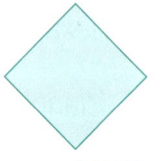

10. 1 x 3 =

MONDAY	TUESDAY	WEDNESDAY	THURSDAY	FRIDAY
Maths	Maths	English	English	English
B	R	E	A	K
English	English	Maths	Maths	Maths
L	U	N	C	H
Science	P.E.	History	Art	RE
Science	Music	Drama	PSHE	Geography

11. How many Maths lessons are there in one week?
12. Which lesson is after lunch on Tuesday?
13. Which lesson is last on Wednesday?
14. Which two lessons are on a Thursday afternoon?

    _____ and _____

15. Round 184 (nearest 10).
16. Sum of 11 and 9 =
17. Name this 3-D shape.

    c

18. 10 – _____ = 7
19. 7 x 3 =
20. Tick which shape will stack.

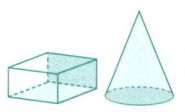

WEDNESDAY

1. _____ to [5:50]
2. 3 x 3 =
3. 150 + 150 =
4. 9 ÷ 3 =
5. Draw a line of symmetry. 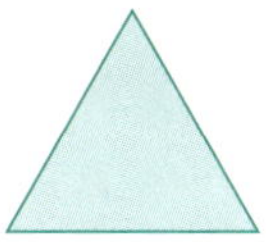
6. 18 ÷ 3 =
7. 3 + 8 =
8. Sum of 9 and 9 =
9. Tick which shape will roll. 
10. Name this 3-D shape.
    c _____ o _____ i _____ 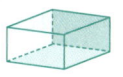
11. 4, 7, 10, _____
12. Draw anticlockwise.

13. £2.55 = _____ p
14. Write four hundred and twelve as a numeral.
15. If you were standing up, would you be vertical or horizontal?

16. 2 metres add 7 metres = _____ metres
17. 11 + 11 + 11 =
18. In 793, what is the meaning of the 7?
    ☐ 700   ☐ 70   ☐ 7
19. 70 + 20 =
20. 10 x 3 =

THURSDAY

1. _____ to [8:40]
2. Which line is horizontal? 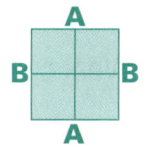
   (a) AA   (b) BB
3. 2 x 3 =
4. Draw a line of symmetry. 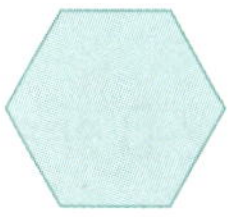
5. Write one hundred and one as a numeral.
6. 30 ÷ 3 =
7. 350 + 350 =
8. 80 minutes = _____ hour(s) _____ minute(s)
9. 1 km = _____ m
10. In 705, what is the place value of the 5?
    ☐ 100s   ☐ 10s   ☐ units
11. Name this 3-D shape. 
12. 12 ÷ 3 =
13. Round 75 (nearest ten).
14. Which is longer, 100 m or 1 km?
15. 9 x 3 =
16. Tom and Ray rode 5 km to school and then rode home. How many kilometres in total for both riders?
17. 7 + 8 =
18. What comes next? 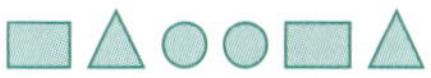
    ■ ▲ ○ ○ ■ ▲
19. 19 − 7 =
20. 21 ÷ 3 =

MONDAY

1. 5 o'clock. 
2. What comes next? 
3. 3 x 4 =
4. Name this 2-D shape. 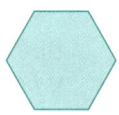
5. 6 + 3 + 5 =
6. Is your pencil ☐ lighter ☐ heavier than 1 kg?
7. Write three hundred and three as a numeral.
8. 18 − 8 =
9. 8 x 4 =
10. Share £10.00 among 5 teachers.
    _____ each
11. 4, 9, 14, _____
12. 400 + 300 =
13. Name this 3-D shape.
    s _____
    p _____ 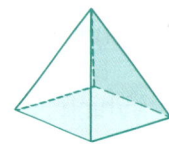
14. 11 − 7 =
15. Sum of 7 and 7 =
16. 90 minutes = _____ hour(s) _____ minute(s)
17. 1 L = _____ mL
18. £2.50 + £0.25 =
19. 9 x 4 =
20. £2.63 = _____ p

TUESDAY

1. Half past 10 
2. 8 ÷ 4 =
3. Name this 3-D shape. 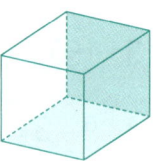
4. 6 + 7 =
5. 20 ÷ 4 =
6. 12 − _____ = 7
7. Do you sleep horizontally or vertically?
8. In 480, what is the place value of the 4?
   ☐ 100s ☐ 10s ☐ units
9. 3, 5, 8, 12, _____
10. 5 x 4 =
11. 100 minutes = _____ hour(s) _____ minute(s)
12. Faces on this pyramid? 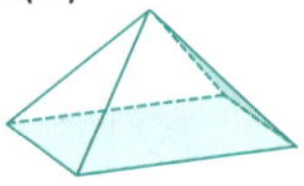
13. £3.49 = _____ p
14. 6 metres and 8 metres = _____ metres
15. £1.50 + £2.50 =
16. 7 x 4 =
17. Is a car ☐ lighter ☐ heavier than 1 kg?
18. 15 − 9 =
19. 250 + 150 =
20. Which is longer?
    (a) 100 cm (b) 10 m (c) 100 m

WEDNESDAY

1. Quarter to 4.
2. Which comes next?

   △ ▽ ⌒ ⌒ ▽

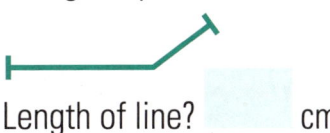

3. 17 − 7 =
4. Faces on this triangular prism?
5. Length of line?   cm 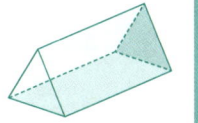
6. 15 −   = 9
7. Sum of 2 and 9 =
8. Are you horizontal or vertical when you walk?
9. 1 kg =   g
10. Is C symmetrical?
11. 5 + 5 + 5 + 5 + 5 =
12. Divide £44.00 between 11 money boxes.

    £   each
13. 65p + 35p =   p
14. £3.50 − £1.50 =
15. Write seven hundred and seventy as a numeral.
16. 410 + 90 =
17. 1 x 4 =
18. 12 ÷ 4 =
19. 1 km =   m
20. 25 + 35 =

THURSDAY

1. Quarter past 8. 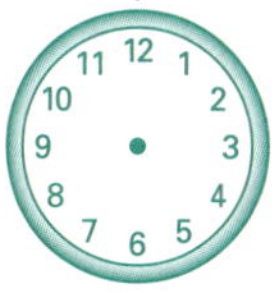
2. 2 x 4 =
3. 16 ÷ 4 =

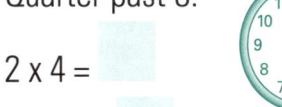

MONDAY	TUESDAY	WEDNESDAY	THURSDAY	FRIDAY
Maths	Maths	English	English	English
B	R	E	A	K
English	English	Maths	Maths	Maths
L	U	N	C	H
Science	P.E.	History	Art	RE
Science	Music	Drama	PSHE	Geography

4. Which lesson is last on Thursday?
5. Which lesson is after lunch on a Wednesday?
6. How many English lessons are there in one week?
7. Which lesson is before lunch on a Friday?
8. Which lesson are there 2 of each week?
9. Faces on this pyramid? 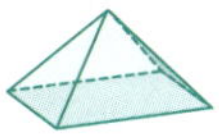
10. Cost of 3 ice-creams at 50p each.
11. Write four hundred and forty as a numeral.
12. 25 + 45 =
13. 18 − 7 =
14. 1 L =   mL
15. Sum of 12 and 9 =
16. 600 − 350 =
17. Is this symmetrical? 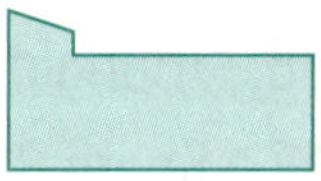
18. 110 minutes =   hour(s)   minute(s)
19. ☐ Clockwise or ☐ anticlockwise? 
20. Which comes next?

    ⬭ ▢ ⬭ ⬭ ▢

MONDAY

1. 10 minutes past 7. 
2. 5 + 7 =
3. 6 + 8 =
4. 6 + 6 =
5. 13 − 9 =
6. 24 − 6 − 6 =
7. If the date is 19.6.06, what is the month?
8. What comes next? 
9. 95 minutes = ___ hour(s) ___ minute(s)
10. Name this 3-D shape. 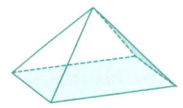
11. Monday is the 19 December. What day will the 22 December be?
12. £7.79 = ___ p
13. Name this 3-D shape. 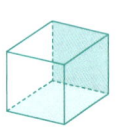
14. What comes after 355?
15. Is a tree ☐ lighter ☐ heavier than 1 kg?
16. Triangle = ___ sides
17. Share 30 apples between 6 people. How many each?
18. Colour half. 
19. 6, 12, ___, 24, 30
20. 17 + 3 = 20, 27 + 3 =

TUESDAY

1. 5 minutes to 4. 
2. 105 minutes = ___ hour(s) ___ minute(s)
3. 14 + 2 = 16, 24 + 2 =
4. 6 + 6 + 6 =
5. What is the chance of you buying ice-cream today?
   ☐ impossible ☐ possible ☐ certain
6. Faces on a cube?
7. Is a teaspoon ☐ lighter ☐ heavier than 1 kg?
8. 3 + 9 =
9. 30 − 6 − 6 =
10. 1 L = ___ mL
11. Name this 3-D shape.

    t

    p 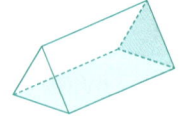
12. 6, 12, 18, ___, 30, 36
13. Share 18 bananas between 6 monkeys. How many each? 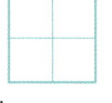
14. Colour $1/4$
15. This is a triangular pyramid. How many faces? 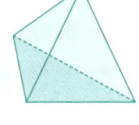
16. What comes after 499?
17. 250 + 650 =
18. Colour $3/4$ 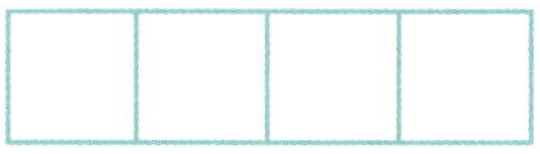
19. Hexagon ___ = sides
20. Square ___ = corners

WEDNESDAY

1. 25 minutes past 8.
2. 18 – ___ = 12
3. |———————|
   Would this line be: ☐ 4 cm ☐ 4 m?
4. What is the chance of you eating pizza for dinner today?
   ☐ impossible ☐ possible ☐ certain
5. What comes next?
   ✏️ 🙂 🙁 ✏️ 🙂
6. 6 + 5 = 
7. 18 – 4 =
8. 14 metres add 7 metres = ___ metres
9. In 859, which number represents the higher value, 5 or 9?
10. On 6.2.06, what is the month?
11. What comes after 709?
12. 115 minutes = ___ hour(s) ___ minute(s)
13. 6 + 6 + 6 + 6 =
14. Share 24 biscuits between 6 people. How many each?
15. Name this regular 2-D shape.
16. Rectangle = ___ corners 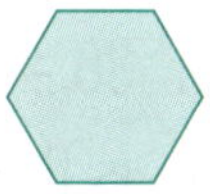
17. Colour $2/4$
18. How many faces on this pyramid?
19. 150 + 450 = 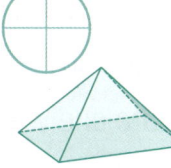
20. Which is heaviest? ☐ 10 g ☐ 1 kg

THURSDAY

1. 20 minutes to 2.
2. 15 + 35 =
3. 600 – 200 =
4. 13 – 7 =
5. Round 609 (nearest hundred).
6. Name this 3-D shape.
7. What is the chance of you going to the beach today? 
   ☐ impossible ☐ possible ☐ certain
8. Share 36 bones between 6 dogs. How many each?
9. 15 – 9 =
10. 60 – 6 – 6 =
11. Faces on a cube?
12. Name this 2-D shape.
13. Which bucket holds more?  
    A 100 mL ☐   B 1 L ☐
14. Milk is £2.00 per litre. How much for 8 litres?
15. If Bob walked along a ladder horizontally, is he going up?
16. 15 + 4 = 19, 25 + 4 =
17. In 276, what is the meaning of the 7?
    ☐ 700 ☐ 70 ☐ 7
18. 6, ___, 18, 24, ___, 36, 42, 48
19. 250 + 150 =
20. Faces on a square pyramid?

Prim-Ed Publishing   www.prim-ed.com   New wave mental maths

MONDAY

1. 10 minutes to 6.
2. 3 × 6 =
3. 9 + 8 =
4. 24 − ___ = 16
5. 6 ÷ 6 =
6. 135 minutes = ___ hour(s) ___ minute(s)
7. Halve 100.
8. Semicircle = ___ sides
9. 30 ÷ 6 =
10. Colour 1/8 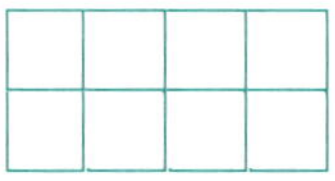
11. Would you buy a kilogram or a centimetre of sugar?
12. 900 − 250 =
13. Is 5 symmetrical?
14. What comes after 885?
15. Date is Tuesday 1 November. What day will the 4th be?
16. 18 − 9 =
17. 3, 6, 10, 15, ___
18. 2.7.06 What is the month?
19. Plot the data on the graph.

Favourite fruit
apple 5
banana 4
orange 2
kiwi 3

20. 9 × 6 =

TUESDAY

1. 5 minutes past 10.
2. 8 + 6 =
3. Name this shape.
4. £1.50 + £0.50 =
5. Colour 3/8 
6. 2 × 6 =
7. 1 m = ___ cm
8. Name this 3-D shape. 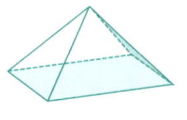
9. Sum of 17 and 7 =
10. Plot the data on the graph.

Favourite colours
red 1
blue 5
yellow 4
green 3

11. 130 minutes = ___ hour(s) ___ minute(s)
12. £3.50 + £6.50 =
13. Colour 1/10 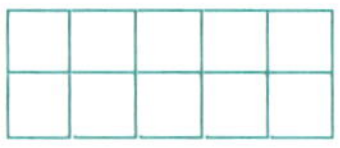
14. 36 ÷ 6 =
15. Is this a ☐ regular or ☐ irregular shape? 
16. In 410, 1 has a value of ___.
17. Halve 90.
18. Date one week before 18 February is ___
19. 10 × 6 =
20. 1 kg = ___ g

WEDNESDAY

1. 25 minutes to 3. 
2. 12 + 8 =
3. 28 – ☐ = 22
4. 4 x 6 =
5. The date is Thursday, 7 January. What day will the 10th be?
6. 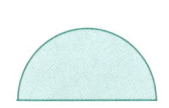 Name this 2-D shape.
7. Sum of 14 and 6 =
8. 24 ÷ 6 =
9. £9.52 =   p
10. Colour $^3/_{10}$ 
11. 15 metres add 14 metres =   m
12. Faces on a cube?
13. 145 minutes =   hour(s)   minute(s)
14. Double 15.
15. What comes after 998?
16. 15 + 25 =
17. Colour $^6/_8$ 
18. £2.50 + £7.50 =
19. This is a triangular pyramid. How many faces? 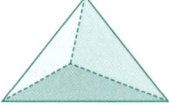
20. 8 x 6 =

THURSDAY

1. 20 minutes past 12. 
2. 6 x 6 =
3. Sum of 2 and 9 =
4. 6 + 6 + 6 + 6 =
5. £9.99 =   p
6. 60 ÷ 6 =
7. Double 35.
8. Colour $^5/_8$ 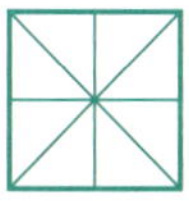
9. Will a square tessellate?
10. Faces on a triangular prism?
11. 300 cm =   m
12. What comes after 629?
13. Plot the data on the graph.

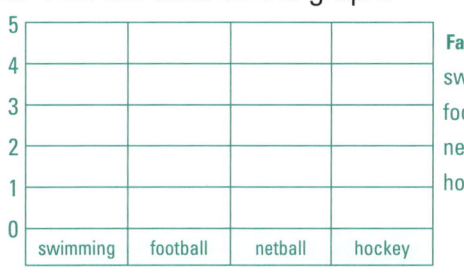

   Favourite sports
   swimming 4
   football 4
   netball 3
   hockey 2

14. £100.00 – £35.00 = £
15. 12 ÷ 6 =
16. 1 km =   m
17. In 387, 3 has the meaning of
18. Colour $^5/_{10}$ 
19. 7 x 6 =
20. Name this shape.

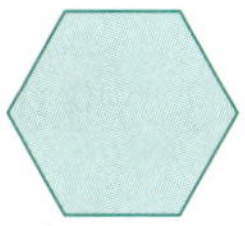

MONDAY

1. 8 o'clock ☐ : ☐
2. 6 + 9 = 
3. Colour $^9/_{10}$
4. £2.00 + £2.50 =
5. 800 – 150 =
6. Colour $^4/_8$ 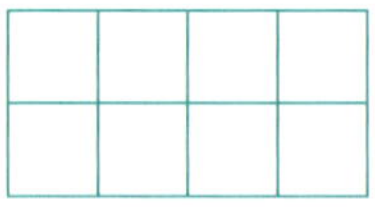
7. 2 x 3 =
8. Faces on a cube?
9. Name this 3-D shape. 
10. 3 x 6 =
11. 6 + 6 + 6 =
12. What number comes after 340?
13.   2 3 1
      + 1 4 2
14. What comes next? 
15. 17 December. What will the date be one week later?
16. £1.00 – 35p =
17. 12 ÷ 3 =
18. £9.05 =   p
19. Write as a fraction. 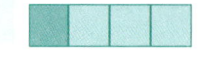
20. 5 x 4 =

TUESDAY

1. Quarter past 11 ☐ : ☐
2. Difference between 12 and 6.
3. 8 x 6 =
4. Triangle =   sides
5. 26 – 8 =
6. 3 + 8 =
7. Write as a fraction. 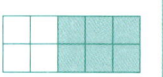
8. 31 metres add 26 metres =   m
9. Write two hundred and thirty as a numeral.
10. Round 245 to the nearest 100.
11. Name this 3-D shape.

    t

    p 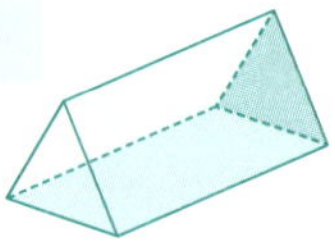
12. 20 ÷ 4 =
13. Which shape will tessellate?
        A   B 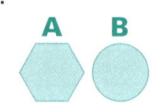
14. 1 kg =   g
15. Colour $^8/_{10}$ 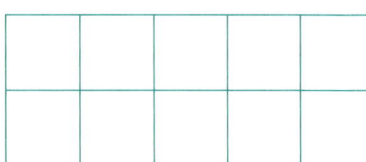
16. 4, 9, 14,
17. £5.00 – £1.50 =
18. What is the chance of the sky falling today?
    ☐ impossible ☐ possible ☐ certain
19. 30 ÷ 3 =
20. 3 x 4 =

WEDNESDAY

1. Quarter to 6   :
2. 22 + 50 =
3. Difference between 18 and 8.
4. £8.20 =   p
5. 6 x 3 =
6. Hexagon =   sides
7. Round 420 (nearest hundred).
8. 6 x 6 =
9. 4 + 4 + 4 + 4 =
10.   3 0 2
      + 5 8 4
11. Colour $^6/_{10}$ 
12. 21 metres add 9 metres =   metres
13. Clockwise or anticlockwise? 
14. Name this 3-D shape.
      c   i d 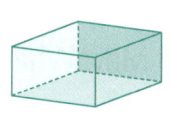
15. £5.00 + £4.75 =
16. 650 + 150 =
17. What comes next? 
18. 21 ÷ 3 =
19. 8 x 4 =
20. £1.00 – 45p =

THURSDAY

1. Quarter past 10   :
2. Difference between 14 and 6.
3. 8 x 5 =
4. Semicircle =   sides
5. 24 – 8 =
6. 4 + 8 =
7. Write as a fraction. 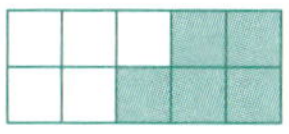
8. 33 metres add 26 metres =   m
9. Write four hundred and thirty as a numeral.
10. Round 375 to the nearest 100.
11. Name this 3-D shape.
    t
    p 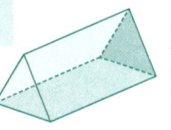
12. 20 ÷ 5 =
13. Which shape will not tessellate? 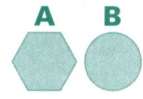
      A B
14. 2 kg =   g
15. Colour $^7/_{10}$ 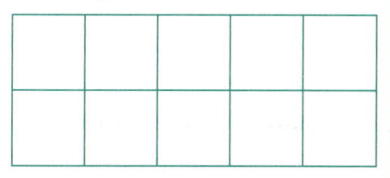
16. 6, 11, 16,
17. £6.00 – £1.50 =
18. What is the chance of a pig flying to the moon?
    ☐ impossible ☐ possible ☐ certain
19. 30 ÷ 2 =
20. 3 x 5 =

MONDAY

1. 5 minutes past 6. ☐ : ☐
2. Draw a six-sided 2-D shape.
3. ☐ L = 1000 mL
4. 5 + 9 =
5. Faces on a cube?
6. Which is heavier, a gram or a kilogram?
7. 7 + 7 + 7 =
8. Share 14 biscuits between 7 dogs. How many each?
9. 3, 6, 9,
10. 7, 14,   , 28, 35
11. £4.00 + £3.50 =

Bus timetable	Bus 1	Bus 2	Bus 3
Parkland	9.00 am	12.15 pm	4.30 pm
Somerton	9.20 am	12.35 pm	4.50 pm
Barksby	9.35 am	12.50 pm	5.05 pm
Denton	9.50 am	1.05 pm	5.20 pm
Carey	10.00 am	1.15 pm	5.30 pm

12. How many buses a day go from Parkland to Carey?
13. What time is the last bus from Barksby to Carey?
14. You need to be in Somerton by 10.00 am. What bus do you catch from Parkland?
15. How many minutes does the bus from Denton to Carey take?
16. 2 x 0 =
17. 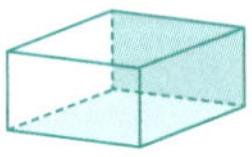 How many faces?
18. Shaded area =   squares 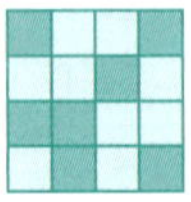
19. What is the chance of you sneezing today?
    ☐ impossible ☐ possible ☐ certain
20. 21 – 7 – 7 =

TUESDAY

1. 20 minutes past 11. ☐ : ☐
2. Draw a rectangle.
3. How many faces? 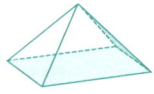
4. In 341, what is the place value of the 3?
    ☐ 100s ☐ 10s ☐ units
5. 1 m =   cm
6. Round 645 (nearest 100).
7. Sum of 3 and 9 =
8. Shaded area =   squares 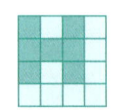
9. 8 + 8 + 8 =
10. 7, 14, 21,   , 35
11. Cost of buying 4 m of rope at £3.00 per metre.
12. How many corners? 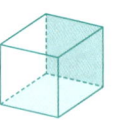
13. £1.00 – 50p =
14. 4, 8, 12,
15. 18 May. What will the date be in one week?
16. Is ½ the same as ²⁄₄?
17. How many triangles can you find? 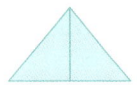
18. 7 + 7 + 7 + 7 =
19. Share 21 balloons between 7 children. How many each? =
20. 20 – 9 =

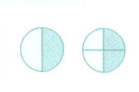

WEDNESDAY

1. 10 minutes to 2.   ☐ : ☐
2. Semicircle = ____ sides 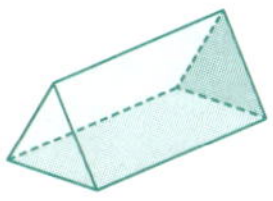
3. How many faces?
4. 5 cm add 12 cm = ____ cm
5. 5 x 0 = 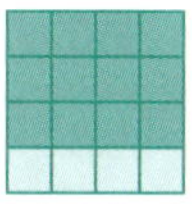
6. Shaded area = ____ squares
7. 28 – 7 – 7 =
8. What is the chance of you eating a piece of fruit today?
   ☐ impossible ☐ possible ☐ certain
9. Share 28 balloons between 7 children. How many each?
10. How many triangles can you find? 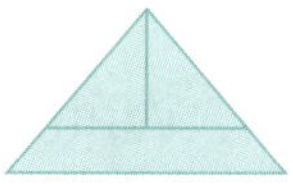
11. 7, 14, 21, 28, ____, 42
12. £2.00 – £1.25 =
13. 5, 10, 15, ____
14. £3.55 = ____ p 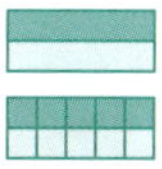
15. Is ½ the same as ⁵/₁₀?
16. 12 – 9 =
17. Will a square tessellate?
18. Name this 2-D shape. 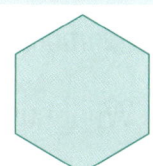
19. 1000 g = ____ kg
20. 4 + 8 + 5 =

THURSDAY

1. 25 minutes to 12.   ☐ : ☐
2. 22 + 5 = 27, so 32 + 5 =
3. How many faces? 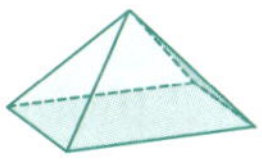
4. 600 cm = ____ m
5. £5.10 = ____ p
6. Perimeter = ____ m 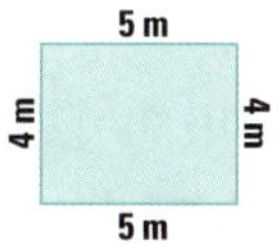
7. 18 – 6 =
8. Shaded area = ____ squares 
9. Share 70 sweets between 7 children. How many each?
10. 7 + 7 + 7 + 7 =
11. Write as a fraction. 
12. 3, 6, 9, 12, ____
13. 7, ____, 21, 28, 35
14. 10 x 0 =
15. How many triangles? 
16. Is ½ the same as ³/₄?
17. What comes after 398?
18. £2.00 – £1.70 =
19. Is ◇ symmetrical?
20. 7 + 4 + 5 =

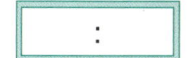

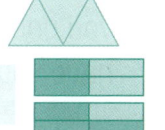

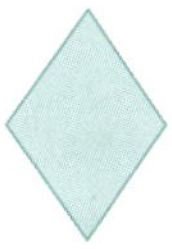

MONDAY

1. 10 minutes past 8.   ☐ : ☐
2. 4 + 7 =
3. What month is 14.8.06?
4. 40 + 80 =
5. Is $1/2$ the same as $4/8$? 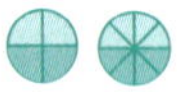
6. Will a cylinder roll?
7. Name this 3-D shape. 
8. Write four hundred and thirty-four as a numeral.
9. Will a cylinder stack?
10. Round 851 (nearest 100).
11. How many surfaces? 
12. 93, 92, 91,
13. Difference between 12 and 8.
14. If a block of chocolate has 20 pieces and you bought 2 blocks, how many pieces have you?
15. 1 x 7 =
16. ___ km = 1000 m
17. 1 L = ___ mL
18. 5 m = ___ cm
19. 28 ÷ 7 =
20. 6 x 7 =

TUESDAY

1. 25 minutes past 10.   ☐ : ☐
2. 13 − 9 =
3. Shaded area = ___ squares 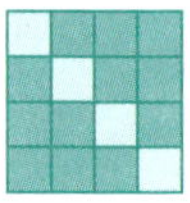
4. 60 + 50 =
5. How many faces? 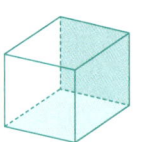
6. Is $1/2$ the same as $7/10$? 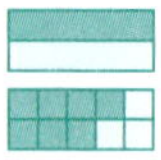
7. How many squares can you find? 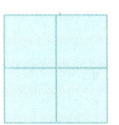
8. 5 x 7 =
9. 4 x 0 =
10. Round 949 (nearest 100).
11. Write as a fraction. 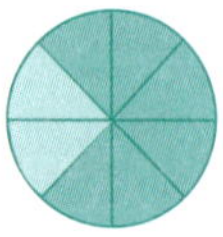
12. Halve 98.
13. 1, 3, 6, 10,
14. 21 ÷ 7 =
15. What direction? 
16. Difference between 16 and 9 =
17. What chance is there of your pencil needing sharpening today?
    ☐ impossible ☐ possible ☐ certain
18. What number comes after 369?
19. 350 + 450 =
20. 4 x 7 =

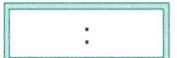

WEDNESDAY

1. 5 minutes to 5.
2. 5 + 8 =
3. How many squares can you find? 
4. 400 + ___ = 600
5. 2 x 7 =
6. Write three hundred and three as a numeral.
7. How many faces? 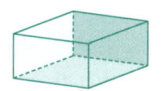
8. 21 – 3 =
9. Double 43.
10. 20, 18, 16,
11. 10 x 7 = 
12. Will this shape tessellate?
13. What number comes after 399?
14. Difference between 100 and 30 =
15. 200 – 70 =

Bus timetable	Bus 1	Bus 2	Bus 3
Parkland	9.00 am	12.15 pm	4.30 pm
Somerton	9.20 am	12.35 pm	4.50 pm
Barksby	9.35 am	12.50 pm	5.05 pm
Denton	9.50 am	1.05 pm	5.20 pm
Carey	10.00 am	1.15 pm	5.30 pm

16. What time does the last bus of day leave Parkland?
17. How long does the bus from Somerton to Barksby take?
18. At what times does the bus leave Denton? ___ , ___ and ___
19. How long does the journey from Parkland to Carey take altogether?
20. In 976, what is the place value of the 7?
    ☐ 100s ☐ 10s ☐ units

THURSDAY

1. 20 minutes to 3.
2. 15 + 65 =
3. 80 + 50 =
4. 6 + 8 =
5. £9.99 = ___ p
6. 300 + ___ = 800.
7. Draw a horizontal line.
8. Will a cone roll?
9. 3 x 7 =
10. Halve 70.
11. How many squares can you find? 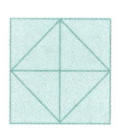
12. 15 cm add 8 cm = ___ cm
13. What number comes after 825?
14. 14 ÷ 7 =
15. 8 x 7 =
16. Name this 2-D shape. 
17. Is $\frac{1}{2}$ the same as $\frac{1}{4}$? 
18. 3 x 0 =
19. If the date is Tuesday, 18 October, what day will 21 October be?
20. 1 kg = ___ g

MONDAY

1. Quarter to 2.   ☐ : ☐
2. 8, 16, ____, 32, 40
3. 25 + 65 =
4. £8.54 = ____ p
5. 3, 7, 11, 15, ____
6. 60 + 60 =
7. Make the largest number using all these digits.
   7, 3, 8
8. Would a tonne of bricks weigh more than a tonne of marshmallows?
9. 200 + ____ = 500
10. 150 − 80 =
11. 8 L = ____ mL
12. 1 $\frac{1}{2}$ hours = ____ hour(s) ____ minute(s)
13. How many corners on a cone? 
14. Write as a fraction. 
15. How many faces on a square pyramid? 
16. Is $\frac{2}{4}$ the same as $\frac{5}{10}$? 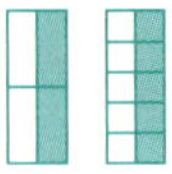
17. Hexagon = ____ sides
18. 8 + 8 + 8 =
19. Write seven hundred and nineteen as a numeral.
20. How many faces on a cube?

TUESDAY

1. 5 minutes past 6.   ☐ : ☐
2. 6 + 7 =
3. Share 16 oranges between 8 children. How many each?
4. 18 − 9 =
5. 70 + 80 =
6. 1 $\frac{1}{4}$ hours = ____ hour(s) ____ minute(s)
7. Make the largest number using all these digits. 0, 5, 3
8. £5.50 = ____ p
9. 1 L = ____ mL
10. What is the chance of you walking home today?
    ☐ impossible ☐ possible ☐ certain
11. 8, 16, 24, ____, 40
12. Is this a regular or irregular shape? 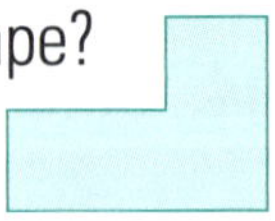
13. 800 − 750 =
14. What direction? 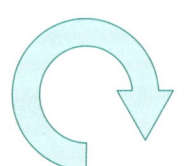
15. 250 + 350 =
16. Name this 3-D shape. 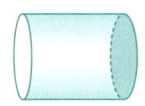
17. £4.00 − £2.40 =
18. 24 − 8 − 8 =
19. 8 + 8 + 8 + 8 =
20. 100 + ____ = 700

WEDNESDAY

1. 25 minutes to 8. ☐ : ☐
2. £9.90 = ☐ p
3. 13 + 8 =
4. 8, 16, 24, 32, ☐ , 48
5. Difference between 10 and 7 =
6. Is $3/4$ the same as $1/2$? 
7. $1\,3/4$ hours = ☐ hour(s) ☐ minute(s)
8. What number comes after 220?
9. 16 cm add 8 cm = ☐ cm
10. Write two hundred and two as a numeral.
11. Name this shape. 
12. Share 24 books between 8 children. How many each?
13. How many faces on this prism? 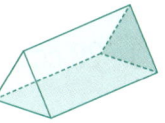
14. 3, 5, 4, 6, 5,
15. How many corners on a cuboid? 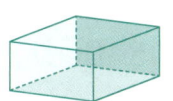
16. In 284, what is the meaning of the 8?
17. Will a cuboid stack?
18. Draw a horizontal line.
19. Is N symmetrical?
20. £8.00 – £3.50 =

THURSDAY

1. 20 minutes past 11. ☐ : ☐
2. 8 + 9 =
3. How many corners on this prism? 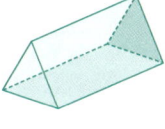
4. 13 – 7 =
5. 14 – 8 =
6. 300 + ☐ = 800
7. Sum of 20 and 90 =
8. $2\,1/2$ hours = ☐ hour(s) ☐ minute(s)
9. What number comes after 809?
10. 8 + 8 + 8 + 8 + 8 =
11. Name this 2-D shape.
12. 600 – 350 =
13. Difference between £1.00 and 75p =
14. Share 40 chocolates among 8 people. How many each?
15. 130, 100, 70, ☐ , 10
16. What fraction of this shape is coloured? 
17. Is Z symmetrical?
18. £2.50 + £0.50 =
19. Shaded area = ☐ squares 
20. Halve 28.

MONDAY

Train timetable				
Depford	8.20 am	11.40 am	3.10 pm	7.15 pm
Chooton	8.35 am	11.55 am	3.30 pm	7.30 pm
Sixby	8.45 am	12.05 pm	3.45 pm	7.40 pm
Onslow	9.05 am	12.25 pm	4.10 pm	8.00 pm
Gurnley	9.10 am	12.40 pm	4.20 pm	8.05 pm
Fedmouth	9.30 am	1.00 pm	4.50 pm	8.25 pm

1. How many trains a day run from Depford to Fedmouth?
2. What time is the first train from Sixby?
3. You need to be in Gurnley by 5 pm. What time do you need to catch a train from Chooton?
4. How long does the first train take to get from Depford to Onslow?
5. 300 − 60 =
6. Name this 3-D shape. 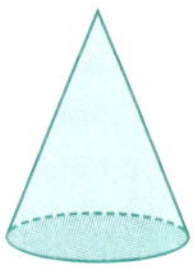
7. 16 ÷ 8 =
8. Is H symmetrical?
9. 1 x 8 =
10. Complete the last two dots in this pattern. 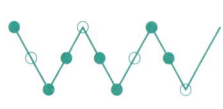
11. 150 − 90 =
12. 6 x 8 =
13. 70 − 40 =
14. 500 + ____ = 900
15. Measure this line. ____ cm 
16. 1 km = ____ m
17. Sum of 50 and 20 =
18. What is the chance of it raining today?
    ☐ impossible ☐ possible ☐ certain
19. 5 x 8 =
20. How many corners?

TUESDAY

1. 45 min. = ____ hour(s) ____ minute(s)
2. 80 + 60 =
3. Will this tessellate? 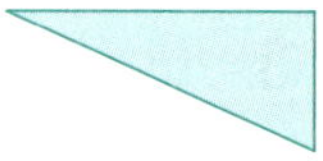
4. Share 12 blocks of chocolate with 4 people. ____ each
5. 24 ÷ 8 =
6. Write one hundred and ninety as a numeral.
7. 7 x 8 =
8. £3.30 = ____ p
9. 64 ÷ 8 =
10. Which holds more water?
    ☐ 1 L bucket
    ☐ 100 mL bucket
11. Difference between 19 and 8 =
12. Name this 3-D shape. 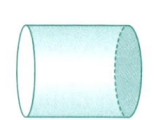
13. 20 cm add 9 cm = ____ cm
14. Round 842 (nearest 10).
15. Draw a line of symmetry. 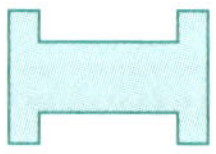
16. Which fraction is smallest; $\frac{1}{2}$ or $\frac{1}{4}$?
17. In 569, the meaning of 6 is ____.
18. 1 kg = ____ g
19. 120 − 50 =
20. 4 x 8 =

WEDNESDAY

1. 2 $\frac{1}{4}$ hours =   hour(s)   minute(s)
2. 3 x 8 =
3. 50 + 90 =
4. Seconds in 3 minutes =
5. 10 m =   cm 
6. How many surfaces on a cone?
7. Double 45.
8. 35 + 45 =
9. Shade $\frac{3}{4}$. 
10. 80 ÷ 8 =
11. 3 m =   cm
12. £10.00 – £6.50 =
13. Draw a line of symmetry. 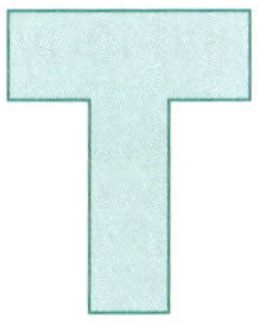
14. 32 ÷ 8 =
15. Halve 28.
16. 120 – 80 =
17. Plot the data on the graph.

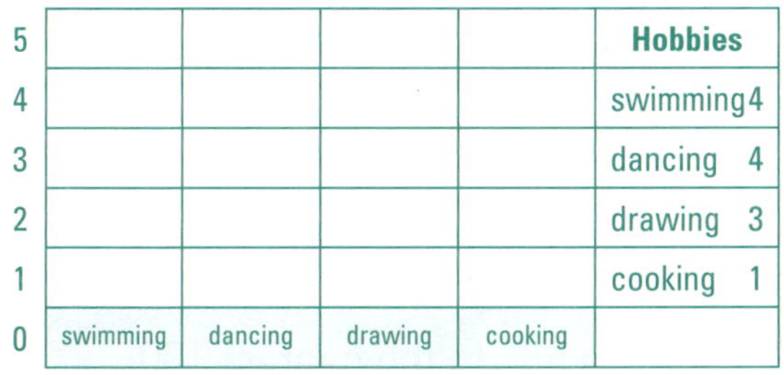

Hobbies	
swimming	4
dancing	4
drawing	3
cooking	1

18. How many children altogether like swimming and dancing?
19. How many more children like dancing than drawing?
20. Which was the least popular hobby?

THURSDAY

1. 2 $\frac{1}{2}$ hours =   hour(s)   minute(s)
2. 2 x 8 =
3. 7 + 8 =
4. How many surfaces on a solid cylinder?
5. 140 – 80 =
6. Name this 2-D shape. 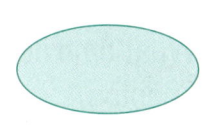
7. 56 ÷ 8 =
8. Hexagon =   sides
9. 6 x 0 =
10. Difference between 15 and 9 =
11. Which fraction is smallest; $\frac{1}{2}$ or $\frac{1}{10}$?
12. How many hours in 2 days?
13. 40 ÷ 8 =
14. £5.00 – £1.50 = £
15. Use a colour to trace over the vertical line. 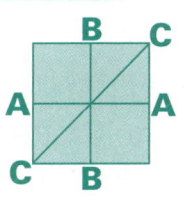
16. Will a cube stack?
17. 8 + 5 + 4 =
18. £8.05 =   p
19. What is the chance of your class having a new pupil this year?
    ☐ impossible ☐ possible ☐ certain
20. 10 x 8 =

MONDAY

1. What time is the last train from Gurnley?

Train timetable				
Depford	8.20 am	11.40 am	3.10 pm	7.15 pm
Chooton	8.35 am	11.55 am	3.30 pm	7.30 pm
Sixby	8.45 am	12.05 pm	3.45 pm	7.40 pm
Onslow	9.05 am	12.25 pm	4.10 pm	8.00 pm
Gurnley	9.10 am	12.40 pm	4.20 pm	8.05 pm
Fedmouth	9.30 am	1.00 pm	4.50 pm	8.25 pm

2. Does the 2nd train take 20 minutes to get from Sixby to Onslow?

3. You need to be in Fedmouth by 1.30 pm. What time do you catch a train from Chooton?

4. How long does the 1st train take to get from Depford to Fedmouth?

    hour(s)   minute(s)

5. Is the 3rd train faster than the 1st train?

6. What is the chance of you eating turkey for lunch?
   ☐ impossible ☐ possible ☐ certain

7. $100 - 35 =$

8. $650 + 150 =$

9. 9, 18, ____, 36

10. $17 - 7 =$

11. How many corners?

12. Share 18 rattles between 9 babies. How many each?

13. $7 \times 0 =$

14. $1 L =$ mL

15. $15 + 15 =$

16. $1 kg =$ g

17. $36 - 9 - 9 =$

18. $3 + 7 + 3 + 7 =$

19. How many faces on a cube?

20. $9 + 9 + 9 =$

TUESDAY

1. $1\frac{3}{4}$ hours =   hour(s)   minute(s)

2. $3 + 9 =$

3. $9 + 9 + 9 + 9 =$

4. £1.00 – 55p =

5. $27 - 9 - 9 =$

6. What is the chance of you winning an award in assembly this term?
   ☐ impossible ☐ possible ☐ certain

7. Share 36 carrots between 9 rabbits. How many each?

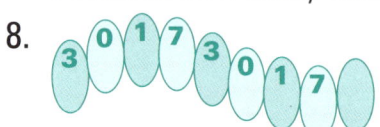

8. 3 0 1 7 3 0 1 7

    Complete the sequence.

9. $12 + 12 + 12 + 12 =$

10. Write five hundred and forty-five as a numeral.

11. The date is 17 March. What will the date be in one week?

12. Measure this line. ⊢——⊣

    ____ cm

13. In 965, what is the place value of the 9?
    ☐ 100s ☐ 10s ☐ units

14. $300 +$ ____ $= 600$

15. Round 651 to the nearest 100.

16. 9, 18, 27, ____, 45

17. Is 6 symmetrical?

18. $35 + 25 =$

19. 22 cm add 6 cm = ____ cm

20. $500 - 90 =$

WEDNESDAY

1. $2^3/_4$ hours = ____ hour(s) ____ minute(s)
2. £9.05 = ____ p
3. Name this 3-D shape.

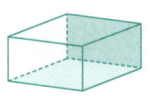

4. 8 + 9 =
5. Write nine hundred and four as a numeral.
6. 4 + 4 + 4 + 4 =
7. How many minutes in one hour?
8. 30, 35, 40,
9. How many faces on a triangular prism?
10. Double 18.
11. Would you be more likely to buy a kilogram or a kilometre of sausages?
12.
    ```
      2 0 3
    + 3 2 4
    ```
13. 40 cm add 18 cm = ____ cm
14. £100.00 – £65.00 =
15. 450 + 150 =
16. 25 + 6 = 31, so 35 + 6 =
17. How many faces on a rectangular prism?
18. Share 45 flowers between 9 vases. How many each?
19. 9, 18, 27, 36, ____ , 54
20. Complete the sequence. 2 3 1 8 __ 3 1 8 2

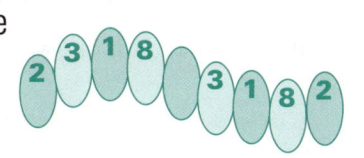

THURSDAY

1. $3^1/_4$ hours = ____ hour(s) ____ minute(s)
2. 7 + 7 =
3. 19 + 5 =
4. Is T symmetrical?
5. 50 – 7 =
6. Name this 3-D shape. 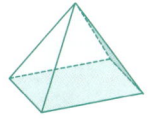
7. 130 – 70 =
8. What is the meaning of the 7 in 703?
9. £1.00 + £2.75 =
10. 21 + 9 = 30, so 31 + 9 =
11. Round 960 (nearest 100).
12. 10 – 6 =
13. 9, 18, 27, 36, 45, 54, ____ , 72, 81, 90
14. Complete the sequence. 5 7 7 5 7 9 7 5
15. 9 + 9 + 9 =
16. Trace the vertical line. 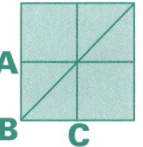
17. Share 72 apples between 9 people. How many each?
18. Would you buy a kilogram or a litre of milk?
19. 45 – 9 – 9 =
20. Shaded area = ____ squares

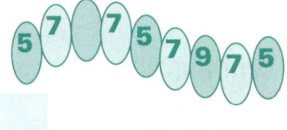

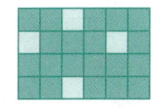

MONDAY

1. 15 cm add 6 cm =   cm
2. 9 + 7 =
3. 15 + 25 =
4. 95 – 9 =
5. 356p = £
6. What day is the 15th?
7. What day is the 30th?
8. How many Fridays are there?
9. What date is the first Tuesday?
10. 3 m =   cm
11. Tick which contains the most.
    ☐ *250 mL beaker*   ☐ *1 litre jug*
12. Will this shape tessellate? 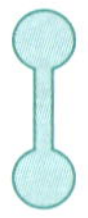
13. Are these parallel?
14. 9 + 8 =
15. 2 x 9 =
16. 36 ÷ 9 =
17. 10, 15, 25, 30, 40

    Rule: add   , then   .
18. What shape are the faces of a cube?
19. Which fraction is the smallest, $\frac{1}{2}$ or $\frac{1}{10}$?
20. Name this 3-D shape.

TUESDAY

1. 21 cm add 7 cm =   cm
2. 4 x 9 =
3. 81 ÷ 9 =
4. Can 20 be divided by 5 equally?
5. 82 – 9 =
6. 8 + 9 =
7. Edges on this square pyramid?
8. Which fraction is the largest, $\frac{1}{2}$ or $\frac{1}{8}$?
9. Write nine hundred and one as a numeral.
10. 452p = £
11. A regular or irregular shape? 
12. What shape are the faces of a cuboid?
13. 97, 94, 91, 88, Rule = subtract
14.   cm = 2 m
15. Name this 3-D shape. 
16. Shade $\frac{3}{4}$. 
17. Tick which contains the least.
    ☐ *500 mL jug*   ☐ *1 litre jug*
18. Shaded area =   squares 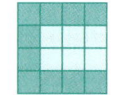
19. Draw $\frac{1}{4}$ turn clockwise. 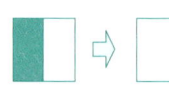
20. You ride your bike 6 km in $\frac{1}{2}$ hour. How long to ride 12 km?

WEDNESDAY

1. 28 cm add 5 cm = ___ cm
2. 9 + 2 + 3 =
3. 90 ÷ 9 =
4. Write six hundred and ten as a numeral.
5. 6 x 9 =
6. What two shapes are the faces of a triangular prism?
   ___ and ___
7. Tick the most likely event:
   ☐ The sun will shine for 2 hours tomorrow.
   ☐ The grass will turn pink.
8. 24 + 16 =
9. £5.00 – £1.80 =
10. Which fraction is the smallest, $1/4$ or $1/10$?
11. 90, 85, 80, 75   Rule:
12. Are these lines parallel?
13. A regular or irregular hexagon?
14. Tick which contains the most.
    ☐ 250 mL jug   ☐ 500 mL jug
15. What shape is a clock face?
16. What is the chance of you wearing brown shoes this week?
    ☐ impossible ☐ not sure ☐ possible
    ☐ might   ☐ certain
17. 350 + 150 =
18. 63 ÷ 9 =
19. 523p = £
20. 3 x 9 =

THURSDAY

1. 31 cm add 12 cm = ___ cm
2. 27 ÷ 9 =
3. Name a six-sided shape.
4. 37 + 13 =
5. 8 + 6 =
6. £3.50 – £1.50 =
7. What is the chance of tomorrow being Friday?
   ☐ impossible ☐ not sure ☐ possible
   ☐ might   ☐ certain
8. Which fraction is the largest, $1/8$ or $1/10$?
9. 45 ÷ 9 =
10. Regular or irregular shape?
11. Round 881 (nearest 100).
12. 8 x 9 =
13. Draw $1/2$ turn right (clockwise).
14. Tick which contains the least.
    ☐ 250 mL jug   ☐ 500 mL jug
15. ___ g = 5 kg
16. 190, 180, 170, 160   Rule:
17. $4 1/2$ m = ___ cm
18. 824p = £
19. Write eight hundred and eleven as a numeral.
20. 10 x 9 =

MONDAY

1. 10 m subtract 3 m = ___ m
2. 2 x 7 =
3. 12 – 7 =
4. 41 + 9 =
5. 3 x 9 =
6. 35 ÷ 7 =
7. Write seven hundred and one as a numeral.
8. How many edges on a cube? 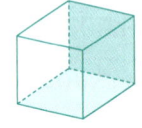
9. 5 x 8 =
10. Name this shape.

11. $4\frac{1}{2}$ L = ___ mL
12. Which fraction is smallest, $\frac{1}{4}$ or $\frac{3}{4}$?
13. Is 2 symmetrical?
14. 824p = £
15. 15 + 35 =
16. What shape are the faces of this pyramid?

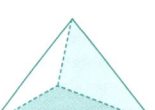

17.  $\frac{1}{4} = \frac{1}{8}$ ☐ true ☐ false

18. 0, 1, 3, 6, 10, ___
19. Tick the most likely event.
    ☐ School will close tomorrow.
    ☐ You will watch TV this week.
20. Tick which contains the most.
    ☐ 1 litre jug
    ☐ 250 mL jug

TUESDAY

1. 16 m – 13 m = ___ m
2. Which fraction is largest, $\frac{1}{2}$ or $\frac{3}{4}$?
3. Write four hundred and eleven as a numeral.
4. 80 ÷ 8 =
5. 926p = £
6. 270 – 120 =
7. Tick which contains the least.
   ☐ 1 litre jug
   ☐ 500 mL jug
8. 6 x 0 =
9. Tick the most likely event.
   ☐ Teacher will fall asleep this afternoon.
   ☐ You will eat lunch. 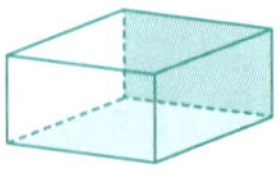
10. 4 x 7 =
11. How many edges on a cuboid?
12. Name this 3-D shape.

13. 400 – ___ = 300
14. 5 x 9 =
15. What shape are the faces of the prism?

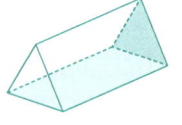

    ___ and ___

16. Round 375 (nearest 100).
17. What shape is a box of cereal?
18. $6\frac{1}{2}$ m = ___ cm
19. Angles on a hexagon?
20. 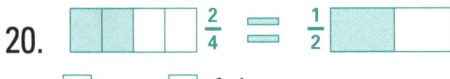 $\frac{2}{4} = \frac{1}{2}$ ☐ true ☐ false

WEDNESDAY

1. 24 m – 4 m = ____ m
2. 6500 g = ____ kg
3. Which fraction is smallest, $^1/_4$ or $^5/_{10}$?
4. Are these lines parallel? 
5. 4 x 8 =
6. 49 – 9 =
7. Shaded area = ____ squares 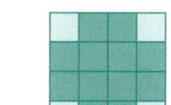
8. 36 ÷ 9 =
9. Draw after a $^3/_4$ turn anticlockwise. 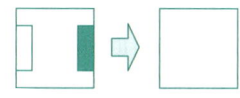
10. 49 ÷ 7 =
11. 6 x 7 =
12. 420 + 180 =
13. 750p = £
14. Double 25.
15. Can this shape tessellate? 
16. 48 + 22 =
17.  ▭ $\frac{1}{2}$ = $\frac{4}{8}$ ▭
    ☐ true   ☐ false
18. What shape is a football?
19. 800 – ____ = 400
20. Tick which contains the most.
    ☐ 500 mL jug   ☐ 250 mL jug

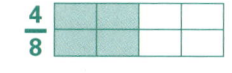

THURSDAY

1. 39 m – 17 m = ____ m
2. What shape is this book?
3. $7^1/_2$ L = ____ mL
4. 34, 29, 24, 19, ____
5. Difference between 20 and 5 =
6. 80 + 30 + 50 =
7.  ▭ $\frac{1}{2}$ = $\frac{6}{10}$ ▭
   ☐ true   ☐ false
8. How many edges on a solid cylinder? 
9. Name this 3-D shape. 
10. 10 x 7 =
11. 500 – ____ = 250
12. 64 ÷ 8 =
13. 8 x 9 =
14. 899p = £
15. Tick the most likely event.
    ☐ It will get dark tonight.
    ☐ A horse will come into your classroom.
16. Sum of 3 and 8 =
17. Write seven hundred and ten as a numeral.
18. £42.00 + £18.00 =
19. Which is the analogue clock? A ☐ B ☐ 
20. Which fraction is largest, $^8/_{10}$ or $^1/_4$?

MONDAY

1. 40 m subtract 20 m = _____ m
2. Round 891 (nearest 10).
3. 400 – _____ = 350
4. Faces on a triangular prism?
5. How many Wednesdays are there?

APRIL
SUN	MON	TUE	WED	THU	FRI	SAT
			1	2	3	4
5	6	7	8	9	10	11
12	13	14	15	16	17	18
19	20	21	22	23	24	25
26	27	28	29	30		

6. What day is the 23rd?
7. What date is the first Sunday?
8. What date is the last Monday?
9. What dates are the Fridays? _____, _____, _____ and _____
10. 35 + 15 =
11. 20 ÷ 10 =
12.   2 3 0
     + 3 4 1

13. 0 x 7 =
14. 9.5 L = _____ mL
15. 15 – 7 =
16. Name a 4-sided shape.
17. Tick the least likely event.
    ☐ I will turn into a sheep.
    ☐ I will read today.
18. Halve 32.
19. 250 mL add 250 mL = _____ mL
20. Write these fractions on the number line.
    $\frac{1}{2}, \frac{1}{4}, \frac{1}{10}$

    0 ↑   ↑   ↑   1

TUESDAY

1. 38 m subtract 14 m = _____ m
2. Are these parallel? 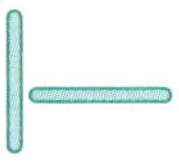
3. 0 x 2 =
4. Tick the least likely event.
    ☐ I will go outside.
    ☐ I will grow a beard tonight.
5. Write five hundred and five as a numeral.
6. Round 487 (nearest 10).
7. 15 – 9 =
8. Edges on a triangular prism? 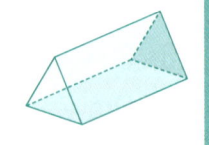
9. Name this 3-D shape. 
10. 900 – _____ = 450
11. 250p = £
12. 8 + 8 + 8 =
13. $5\frac{1}{2}$ m = _____ cm
14. 8 x 4 =
15.   4 0 6
     + 2 7 2

16. £5.00 – £1.50 =
17. $\frac{1}{4} = \frac{3}{8}$ ☐ true ☐ false
18. 140 + 160 =
19. Draw anticlockwise.
20. Shaded area = _____ squares

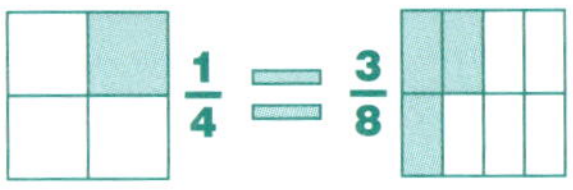

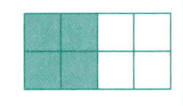

46 New wave mental maths www.prim-ed.com Prim-Ed Publishing

WEDNESDAY

1. 45 m – 15 m = ____ m
2. 310p = £ ____
3. 69 + 21 =
4. 500 mL add 250 mL = ____ mL
5. 3 x 8 =
6. 600 – ____ = 300
7. 5 x 4 =
8. 0 x 10 =
9. 7000 g = ____ kg
10. What is the chance of tomorrow being Saturday?
    ☐ impossible ☐ not sure ☐ possible
    ☐ might ☐ certain
11. How many edges on a triangular prism? 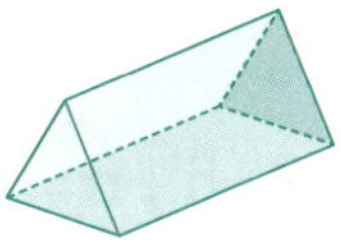
12. 6 x 3 =
13. 6 + 7 =
14. Total cost of buying 10 sheets of paper at 10p each?
15.   8 3 1
      + 1 4 2
16. 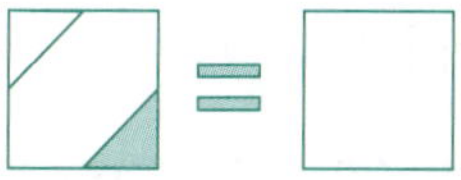 Draw $\frac{1}{2}$ turn clockwise.
17. 50 – 15 =
18. Name this 3-D shape. 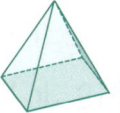
19. 16 – 7 =
20. 3, 9, 14, 18, ____

THURSDAY

1. 100 m subtract 50 m = ____ m
2. 700 – ____ = 400
3. Draw a line of symmetry.
4. 390 – 90 =
5.   3 0 5
    + 4 2 1
6. 41 + 19 =
7. Marty and Jack drank 6 L of water. Marty drank twice as much as Jack. How many litres did Marty drink? ____ litres
8. 0 x 5 =
9. Tick the least likely event.
   ☐ I will visit the moon this week.
   ☐ I will eat a biscuit over the weekend.
10. 625p = £ ____
11. 250 mL add 500 mL = ____ mL
12. Round 475 (nearest 10).
13. Edges on a square pyramid? 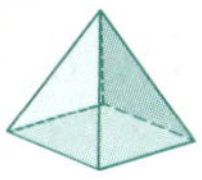
14. Write nine hundred and nine as a numeral.
15. Write nine hundred and ninety as a numeral.
16. Draw $\frac{1}{4}$ turn clockwise. 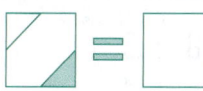
17. Write these fractions on the number line. $\frac{4}{8}, \frac{3}{4}, \frac{2}{10}$ 
18. 150 + 650 =
19. 6 x 4 =
20. £1.00 – £0.30 =

New wave mental maths   47

MONDAY

1. 12 cm − 6 cm =   cm
2. $1\frac{1}{2}$ m =   cm
3. 17 + 5 =
4. 903p = £
5. Kathy and Ray ate 9 pieces of toast. Ray ate 5 pieces. How many pieces of toast did Kathy eat?
6. Tick the least likely event.
   ☐ *Cows will moo.*
   ☐ *Pigs will fly.* 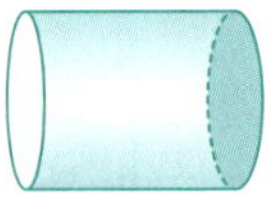
7. Edges on a cylinder?
8. Write eight hundred and fifteen as a numeral.
9. 36 ÷ 6 =
10. Write these fractions on the number line. $\frac{8}{10}, \frac{1}{4}, \frac{5}{8}$

    0 ───↑────↑──↑── 1

11. 8 + 9 =
12. 16 + 4 = 20, so 26 + 4 =
13. 64 + 16 =
14. Shaded area =   squares
15.   8 3 6
        − 5 1 4

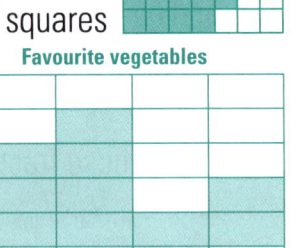

    Favourite vegetables
16. 7 × 5 =
17. How many children liked peas?
18. Which was the most popular vegetable?
19. How many children liked cabbage?
20. How many children chose a favourite vegetable?

TUESDAY

1. 20 cm − 14 cm =   cm
2. 250p = £
3. Write these fractions on the number line. $\frac{7}{10}, \frac{1}{2}, \frac{2}{8}$

   0 ─────↑──↑──↑────── 1

4. 9 × 3 =
5. £2.00 − 30p =
6. 25 + 7 = 32, so 35 + 7 =
7. Draw a $\frac{1}{4}$ turn right. 
8.   9 7 4
       − 2 6 1

9. 6 + 6 =   × 6 = 12
10. Do sets of parallel lines ever meet?
11. What number comes before 499?
12. How many edges on a cube?
13. 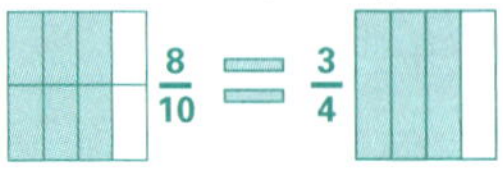 $\frac{8}{10} = \frac{3}{4}$ ☐ *true* ☐ *false*
14. Colour $\frac{1}{4}$ ☐☐☐☐ 
15. Write five hundred and fifty-five as a numeral.
16. Adam has 24 stickers and Fay has 25. How many stickers altogether?
17. 0.1 > 1.0   ☐ *true* ☐ *false*
18. 0.9 < 1.0   ☐ *true* ☐ *false*
19. In 16.8, what is the place value of the 8?
    ☐ *10s* ☐ *units* ☐ *tenths*
20. Tick the least likely event.
    ☐ *You will have an ice-cream today.*
    ☐ *You will have a hot dinner today.*

WEDNESDAY

1. 27 cm – 7 cm = ____ cm
2. 4 x 6 =
3. 11 + 11 + 11 =
4. In 28.5, what is the meaning of the 5?
   ☐ 50 ☐ 500 ☐ 0.5
5. 654p = £
6. What number comes before 301?
7. Surfaces on a solid cylinder?
8. Edges on a cuboid? 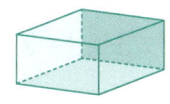
9. 5 + 5 = 2 x 5 =
10. 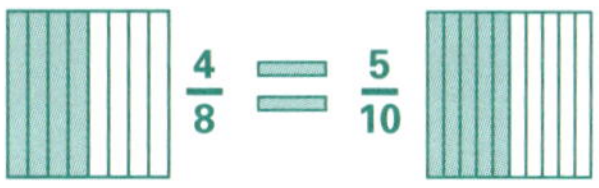 $\frac{4}{8} = \frac{5}{10}$
    ☐ true ☐ false
11. Sam has 33 sweets and Karina has 24. How many sweets altogether?
12. The date a week after 20 April is ____.
13. £5.00 – £1.60 =
14. Colour $\frac{3}{4}$ △△△△
15. 4 + 4 = 2 x 4 =
16. 0.3 < 1 ☐ true ☐ false
17. Tick the least likely event.
    ☐ It will snow on Saturday.
    ☐ It will rain on Saturday.
18. 84 + 6 = 90, so 94 + 6 =
19. 5, 8, 12, 17,
20.   7 4 9
    – 4 2 3

THURSDAY

1. 32 cm – 4 cm = ____ cm
2. 67 + 7 = 74, so 77 + 7 =
3. Draw $\frac{3}{4}$ turn clockwise. 
4. 15 – 8 =
5. 21 ÷ 3 =
6.   8 4 7
   – 2 0 6
7. 8 + 8 = 2 x 8 =
8. What number comes before 890?
9. Edges on a triangular prism? 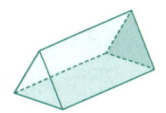
10. Julie has 45p and Stuart has 52p. How much altogether? ____ p
11. Colour $\frac{6}{10}$ ☐☐☐☐☐☐☐☐☐☐
12. 55 + 15 =
13. Write these fractions on the number line.
    $\frac{3}{4}, \frac{4}{8}, \frac{9}{10}$

    0 |—|—|—|—|↑—|—|↑—|↑—| 1
14. 0.4 = 4 ☐ true ☐ false
15. $2\frac{1}{2}$ kg = ____ g
16. Date is Wednesday 9 February. What date will Sunday be?
17. 0.9 = 9 ☐ true ☐ false
18. 880p = £
19. Tick the least likely event.
    ☐ You will learn to drive a car next week.
    ☐ You will be a passenger in a car next week.
20. 7 x 3 =

MONDAY

1. 15 cm subtract 9 cm = ☐ cm
2. 7 + 7 + 7 = 3 x 7 =
3. What number comes before 700?
4. 0.6, 0.7, 0.8,
5.   849
     − 327
6. Colour $^5/_8$ △△△△△△△△
7. 24 + 9 =
8. Can a circle tessellate?
9. Sam has 26p and Kelly has 25p. How much altogether? ☐ p
10. 7 x 6 =
11. 600 − 240 =
12. What is $^1/_2$ of 12?
13. The date a week before 14.10.06?
14. Draw a horizontal line.
15. 8 x 2 = 16 = 4 x
16. Circle the largest: $^1/_2$ or $^3/_4$
17. What is the chance of you not getting any work done today?
    ☐ impossible ☐ not sure ☐ possible
    ☐ might ☐ certain
18. 0.4 < 0.7   ☐ true ☐ false
19. Is a butterfly symmetrical?
20. What is $^1/_2$ of 100?

TUESDAY

1. 50 cm − 25 cm = ☐ cm
2.   765
     − 241
3. 6 x 8 =
4. Sum of 9 and 3 =
5. 45 + 15 =
6. 1.6, 1.7, 1.8,
7. 3 + 3 + 3 = 1 x 9 =
8. What is the chance of you smiling today?
   ☐ impossible ☐ not sure ☐ possible
   ☐ might ☐ certain
9. 5 children shared 40 lollies.
   ☐ each
10. Draw a mirror image.
11. Colour $^3/_8$ ☐☐☐☐☐☐☐☐
12. What is $^1/_2$ of 20?
13. Can this shape tessellate?
14. 5 x 4 = 20 = 2 x
15. Circle the largest. $^4/_8$ or $^6/_{10}$
16. 0.5 > 0.2   ☐ true ☐ false
17. Circle the set of parallel lines.
      A B C D
18. What number comes before 150?
19. Difference between 14 and 8.
20. 0.9 > 0.8   ☐ true ☐ false

WEDNESDAY

1. 79 cm – 12 cm = ____ cm
2. 83 + 9 =
3. 15 – 8 =
4. What is the date before 1st January?

   JANUARY
5. What day is the 30th?
6. How many days in the last week of January?
7. What day will 1st February be?
8. Your birthday is the 3rd. What will the date be one week after this?
9. 4 + 4 + 4 = 3 x 4 =
10.
    $$\begin{array}{r} 6\ 9\ 3 \\ -\ 4\ 5\ 3 \\ \hline \end{array}$$

11. 0.4 > 0.8 ☐ true ☐ false
12. The place value of 7 in 24.7 is ____.
13. Colour $7/10$ ○○○○○○○○○○
14. 3 x 8 =
15. Round 409 (nearest 10).
16. Debbie has 85p and Suzy has 14p. How much altogether? ____ p
17. What is $1/2$ of 60?
18. What is the chance of you eating an ice-cream today?
    ☐ impossible ☐ not sure ☐ possible
    ☐ might ☐ certain
19. What comes before 660?
20. 0.1, 0.2, ____, 0.4, 0.5

THURSDAY

1. 99 cm – 22 cm = ____ cm
2. How many edges on a triangular prism?
3. Circle the largest: $3/4$ or $2/8$
4. 3 x 4 = 12 = 2 x
5. £5.00 – £3.70 =
6.
    $$\begin{array}{r} 8\ 4\ 6 \\ -\ 7\ 2\ 1 \\ \hline \end{array}$$
7. 800 – 370 =
8. £11.50 + £1.50 =
9. What number comes before 999?
10. Liam has 62p and David has 35p. How much altogether? ____ p
11. What is $1/2$ of 28?
12. Name a 6-sided 2-D shape.
13. 65 + 15 =
14. Draw a mirror image (reflection).
15. 37 + 13 =
16. 5 + 5 + 5 = 3 x 5 =
17. 0.3 > 0.4 ☐ true ☐ false
18. 0.6, 0.5, ____, 0.3, 0.2, 0.1
19. Angles in a square?
20. 300 cm = ____ m

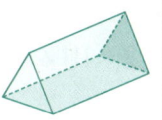

MONDAY

1. 5 kg add 6 kg = _____ kg
2. 10 + 10 + 10 + 10 = 4 x 10 =
3. What number comes before 500?
4. $\frac{1}{10}$ = 0.1 or 1?
5. TVs are £300 and DVDs are £200. How much altogether?
6. Draw a mirror image.
7. 12 x 0 =
8. What is $\frac{1}{4}$ of 8?
9. How many socks in 5 pairs?
10. 4)‾20 =
11. 8 x 5 =
12. 23 + 27 =
13. Name this shape.
14. Faces on above shape?
15. Draw after a $\frac{1}{4}$ turn right.
16. Dennis has 15 stickers and Sid has 9. How many fewer has Sid?
17. 0.5 = 5 ☐ true ☐ false
18. 8 + 8 =
19. Take 8 from 17.
20. What is the chance of you going to the dentist today?
    ☐ impossible ☐ not sure ☐ possible
    ☐ might ☐ certain

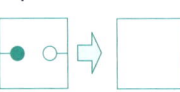

TUESDAY

1. 50 kg + 30 kg = _____ kg
2. 8 + 8 + 8 = 3 x 8 =
3. 87, 81, 75,
4. 620 + 180 =
5. Trousers are £60 and jumpers £35. How much altogether?
6. 30 ÷ 6 =
7. How many eyes on 6 heads?
8. $\frac{3}{10}$ = 3 or 0.3?
9. Name a 6-sided 2-D shape.
10. What number comes before 730?
11. 15 x 1 =
12. Draw a mirror image (reflection).
13. 3 x 8 =
14. Difference between 12 and 7.
15. Circle the smallest, $\frac{3}{8}$ or $\frac{8}{10}$
16. 5)‾25 =
17. What is $\frac{1}{4}$ of 12?
18. 16 + 16 =
19. Bill has 25 sweets and Ben has 19. How many fewer has Ben?
20. What is the chance of you getting a new bike today?
    ☐ impossible ☐ not sure ☐ possible
    ☐ might ☐ certain

WEDNESDAY

1. 26 kg + 23 kg = _____ kg
2. Will this tessellate? 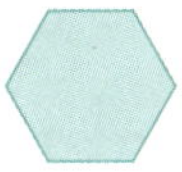
3. 40 ÷ 10 = 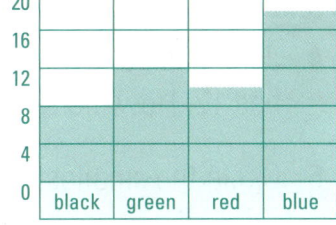
4. 22 x 2 =
5. $^8/_{10}$ = 0.8 or 8?

Favourite colours

6. The least popular colour was
7. How many children liked green?
8. How many children liked blue?
9. Which colour did 10 children like?
10. How many children were asked altogether?
11. Write eighteen point three as a numeral.
12. Round 862 (nearest 100).
13. 47 + 9 =
14. A bike is £250 and a helmet £30. How much altogether?
15. 15 − 9 =
16. What is the chance of the sky falling on your head today?
    ☐ impossible ☐ not sure ☐ possible
    ☐ might ☐ certain
17. Write as a fraction. 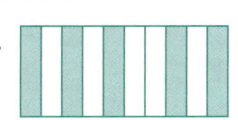
18. 410 + 190 =
19. What number comes before 201?
20. 6 + 6 + 6 + 6 = 4 x 6 =

THURSDAY

1. 84 kg + 15 kg = _____ kg
2. £0.80 + £0.20 =
3. What number comes before 900?
4. 20 ÷ 5 =
5. What is $^1/_4$ of 16?
6. 198, 188, 178,
7. 16 x 0 =
8. A desk is £75 and a chair £25. How much altogether?
9. 8 x 7 =
10. 9 + 9 + 9 = 3 x 9 =
11. Is Z symmetrical?
12. Name this shape. 
13. 2)‾16 =
14. How many toes on 3 feet?
15. 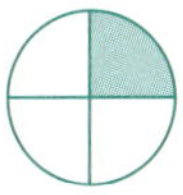 $\frac{1}{4}$ = $\frac{3}{8}$ ☐ true ☐ false
16. Mark where the right angle is located. 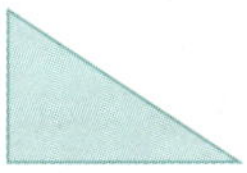
17. What is the chance of you wearing blue socks today?
    ☐ impossible ☐ not sure ☐ possible
    ☐ might ☐ certain
18. Stacey has 38 t-shirts! Clare has 4. How many fewer has Clare?
19. 500 − 220 =
20. Double 35.

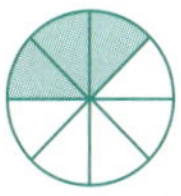

MONDAY

1. 12 kg add 13 kg = ___ kg
2. Halve 50.
3. 13 − 9 = 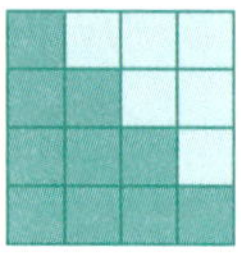
4. Shaded area = ___ squares
5. 3 ÷ 3 =
6. Treble 2 =
7. Sides on a hexagon?
8. £10.00 − £5.30 =
9. $7/10$ = 0.7 or 7?
10. 35 x 0 =
11. How many gloves in 8 pairs?
12. 0.1 > 0.3   ☐ true ☐ false
13. 3 x 4 = 4 x
14. Draw $3/4$ turn clockwise. 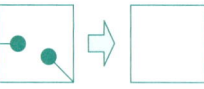
15. 12 + 12 + 12 + 12 =
16. What is $3/4$ of 8?
17. 9 x 6 =
18. 4)‾16 =
19. 20 − 9 =
20. Has a square got parallel sides?

TUESDAY

1. 30 kg + 15 kg = ___ kg
2. Treble 3 =
3. 2 x 4 = 4 x
4. John has 23 toy cars. Fred has 12. How many altogether?
5. Circle the smallest, $3/4$ or $3/8$.
6. Write three point four.
7. 0.5 > 0.8   ☐ true ☐ false
8. Shaded area = ___ squares 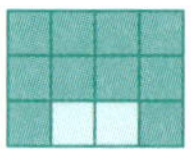
9. 420 + 180 =
10. 16 x 1 =
11. A jacket is £70 and a skirt £25. How much altogether?
12. £2.00 − £1.20 =
13. What shape will you see in the cross-section? 
14. How many ears on 7 heads?
15. 5)‾45 =
16. Name this 3-D shape. 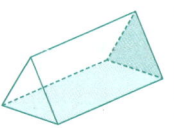
17.  Measure this line. ___ cm
18. 0.2 = $2/10$ or 2?
19. What is $3/4$ of 20?
20. Sum of 80 and 4 =

WEDNESDAY

1. 15 kg + 25 kg =   kg

2. £0.40 + £0.60 =

3. Share 24 strawberries with 3 friends.   each

4. Is N symmetrical?

5. The place value of 6 in 34.6 is   .

6. Draw a mirror image (reflection).

7. 300 – 60 =

8. Treble 4 =

9. 6 x 3 = 3 x

10. Has a triangle got parallel sides?

11. How many toes on 5 feet?

12. 6)30

13. Mark has 14 biscuits. Jane has 33. How many altogether?

14. 6 x 5 =

15. 45 ÷ 9 =

16. A doll is £25 and a teddy bear £30. How much altogether?

17. 18 x 10 =

18. Circle the smallest, $^7/_{10}$ or $^1/_4$.

19. 2 x 8 =

20. What is $^3/_4$ of 40?

THURSDAY

1. 12 kg + 24 kg =   kg

2. A B C
Which has a right-angle?

3. 5 x 3 = 3 x

4. Has a square got parallel sides?

5. What is $^3/_4$ of 12?

6. 14 x 2 =

7. How many days in 5 full weeks?

8. 9)36

9. 27 + 23 =

10. What shape will you see in the cross-section?

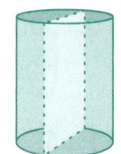

11. The date a week after 27 March?

12. 250 – 150 =

13. How many Saturdays?

DECEMBER						
SUN	MON	TUES	WED	THUR	FRI	SAT
				1	2	3
4	5	6	7	8	9	10
11	12	13	14	15	16	17
18	19	20	21	22	23	24
25	26	27	28	29	30	31

14. What day is the 18th?

15. Circle Christmas Day.

16. What is the date one week before Christmas Day?

17. Sam's birthday is on 14th December. How many days after Sam's birthday is Christmas Day?

18. 7 x 8 =

19. £6.40 + £1.60 =

20. Treble 5 =

MONDAY

1. 12 kg subtract 5 kg = ◻ kg
2. Treble 6 =
3. 2 x 5 = 5 x
4. 6)̄36 =
5. Has a rectangle got parallel sides?
6. 35 + 9 =
7. How many socks in 9 pairs?
8. 5 x 10 =
9. What is $5/10$ of 20?
10. Jack has 59p. Jill has 24p. How much more has Jack? ◻ p
11. 4, 5, 7, 8, 10,
12. 20 x 0 =
13. Circle the smallest, $3/4$ or $7/8$.
14. 16 x 1 =
15. Is this house symmetrical?
16. Double 45.
17. 2 x 8 = 16 = 4 x
18. Write these fractions on the number line. $1/2$, $6/8$, $3/10$
19. How many triangles can you find?
20. How many right angles in a rectangle?

TUESDAY

1. 20 kg – 18 kg = ◻ kg
2. 1, 5, 9, 13, 17,
3. Has a square got parallel sides?
4. 60 + 90 =
5. 8 x 4 = 4 x
6. 7)̄21 =
7. 25 + 15 =
8. Will this tessellate?
9. Treble 7=
10. Write forty-four point six as a numeral.
11. How many days in 4 full weeks?
12. 15 – 8 =
13. 6 x 4 = 24 = 3 x
14. What is $7/10$ of 100?
15. The meaning of the 3 in 12.3 is: ☐ 0.1 ☐ 3 ☐ 0.3
16. Name this shape.
17. Halve 98.
18. A regular or irregular shape?
19. Conor has 88p. Richard has 12p. How much more has Conor? ◻ p
20. £0.90 + £0.10 =

WEDNESDAY

1. 38 kg − 14 kg =   kg
2. 35 + 15 =
3. 16 − 9 = 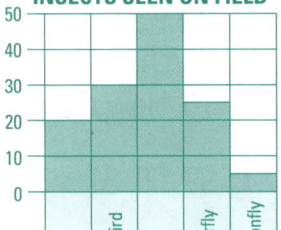
4. How many ladybirds were there?

   INSECTS SEEN ON FIELD (bar chart: bee, ladybird, fly, butterfly, dragonfly)

5. Which insect was there most of?
6. How many more ladybirds than bees were there?
7. Which insect was there 5 of?
8. How many bees and dragonflies altogether?
9. 8)$\overline{64}$ =
10. How many toes on 7 feet?
11. 540 + 160 =
12. 95, 89, 83,
13. 3 x 8 =
14. Faces on a square pyramid? 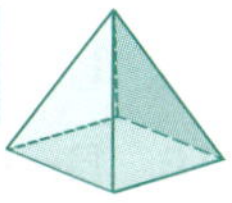
15. Treble 9 =
16. Edges on a triangular pyramid? 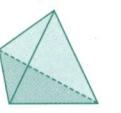
17. 6 x 3 = 3 x
18. Edges on a triangular prism? 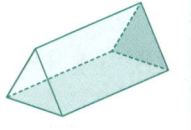
19. Draw a reflection. 
20. £10.00 − £3.30 =

THURSDAY

1. 49 kg − 22 kg =   kg
2. 6 x 4 =
3. Treble 8.
4. Draw 2 parallel lines.
5. 9 x 3 = 3 x
6. Kate has 75p. Paul has 15p. How much more has Kate?   p
7. Edges on a cube? 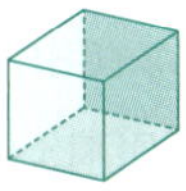
8. Edges on a square pyramid? 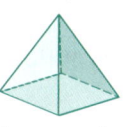
9. Write these fractions on the number line. $\frac{3}{4}$, $\frac{2}{10}$, $\frac{4}{8}$

   0 —————————— 1

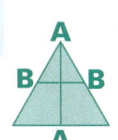

10. Which line is vertical?
11. 500 − 140 =
12. Round 860 (nearest 100).
13. 4)$\overline{24}$ =
14. 19 + 6 =
15. 3 x 10 = 30 = 6 x
16. What is $\frac{5}{10}$ of 50?
17. 13 − 7 =
18. If you ride 5 km in half an hour, how far could you ride in 2 hours?   km
19. 8 x 6 =
20. Has a circle got parallel sides?

MONDAY

1. 18 kg subtract 7 kg =   kg
2. Halve 32.

TV Guide		
Cartoons ...... 6.00 am	News .... 9.00 am	Film .... 10.00 am
News .... 6.30 am	Get fit! .... 9.15 am	Soap opera . 11.30 am
GMTV .... 7.00 am	Cartoons ...... 9.45 am	News .... 11.55 am

3. How many times is the news on?
4. How long is the film?
5. How many minutes are the cartoons on for altogether?
6. How long is 'GMTV' on for?
7. How long is the soap opera?
8. 45 – 9 =
9. How many right angles in a square?
10. 19 x 10 =
11. $5 \overline{)35}$ =
12. Edges on a cone?
13. $\frac{4}{8}$ of 16 =
14. Has a triangle got parallel lines? 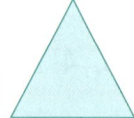
15. Marie has 99p. Andrew has 19p. How much more has Marie?

           p

16. 2, 7, 3, 8, 4, 9,
17. Share 24 cakes between 6 children. How many each?
18. 4 x 7 =
19. 10 x 4 = 4 x
20. Shaded area =   squares

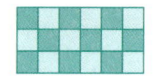

TUESDAY

1. 68 kg – 26 kg =   kg
2. 4 x 9 = 9 x
3. Ben has 24 cakes. Cathy has 10. How many more has Ben?
4. 99, 90, 81,
5. 12 – 7 =
6. Round 649 (nearest 100).
7. 14 x 2 =
8. Share 42 bones between 6 hungry dogs. How many each?
9. Has a semicircle got parallel lines? 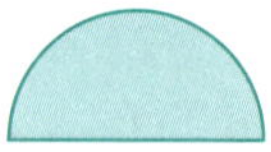
10. £10.00 – £5.50 =
11. How many edges on a cube?
12. How many surfaces on a solid cylinder?
13. 46 + 34 =
14. Write seven hundred and seventy-nine as a numeral.
15. Corners on a cube?
16. Draw $\frac{1}{4}$ turn clockwise. 
17. $\frac{2}{8}$ of 12 =
18. 7 x 8 =
19. $9 \overline{)72}$ =
20. £1.00 – 55p =

WEDNESDAY

1. 87 kg – 14 kg =   kg
2. £2.50 + £4.50 =
3. 65 – 8 =
4. Is this a regular shape? 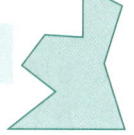
5. 7 x 5 = 5 x
6. 0.4 = 4, 0.1 or $^4/_{10}$?
7. Write a symmetrical letter.
8. 24 x 10 =
9. What 2 shapes make a triangular prism?
                      and
10. 8)‾40 =
11. Has a hexagon got parallel lines? 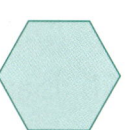
12. $^6/_8$ of 20 =
13. 800 – 170 =
14. 7 x 6 =
15. Share 81 fish between 9 penguins. How many each?
16. The date a week before Christmas Day?

17. 9, 19, 29, 39,
18. Name a 4-sided shape.
19. Fred has 84 stickers. Ken has 73. How many more has Fred?
20. This is a fuel gauge. How much is left in the tank?
    ☐ $^1/_4$ ☐ $^1/_2$ ☐ $^3/_4$

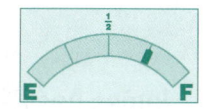

THURSDAY

1. 99 kg – 10 kg =   kg
2. What 2 shapes make a cylinder?
                      and
3. 4 x 6 = 6 x
4. Is a prism 2-D or 3-D?
5. 700 – 200 =
6. 15 + 45 =
7. Write sixty-two point eight as a numeral.
8. 8 x 9 =
9. Measure this line. ├────────┤
           cm
10. Difference between 14 and 8.
11. 30 + 80 =
12. If you walked 3 km in 30 minutes, how far would you walk in an hour?
           km
13. Share 64 crayons between 8 boys. How many each?
14. Draw a reflection. 
15. Has a rectangle got parallel lines?
16. Laura has £85. Josh has £25. How much more has Laura?
17. How much left in the tank? 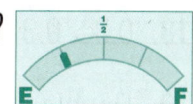
18. 25 x 1 =
19. 14 – 7 =
20. Snoopy has 76 bones. Lassie has 42. How many more has Snoopy?

MONDAY

1. 6 g add 18 g = ___ g
2. 8 x 5 = 5 x
3. Write a symmetrical number.
4. 7 x 4 =

TV Guide		
News........... 6.00 pm	Film............... 8.00 pm	Football ...... 10.30 pm
Pop chart ...... 7.00 pm	News.......... 10.00 pm	Film............. 11.00 pm
Coronation Street............7.30 pm		News.......... 12.45 am

5. How many films are on?
6. How long is 'Coronation Street' on for?
   ___ minutes
7. How many times is the news on?
8. How long is the 2nd film on for?
9. How long are both films on for altogether?
10. What is on at 7 o'clock?
11. Round 750 (nearest 100).
12. 15 – 6 =
13. 8 + 4 =
14. Measure this line.
    ___ cm
15. Draw a reflection of 4
16. 12 x 10 =
17. 0.1, 0.2, 0.3, ___, 0.5
18. 0.3 > 0.9 ☐ true ☐ false
19. Double 45.
20. Name this shape.

TUESDAY

1. 25 g + 50 g = ___ g
2. 6 x 9 = 9 x
3. 68 + 22 =
4. 5)̄40 =
5. 0.3 < 0.7 ☐ true ☐ false
6. 8 x 3 =
7. Is a cube 2-D or 3-D?
8. 8 x 5 =
9. Share 45 nuts between 9 squirrels. How many each?
10. Has a square got parallel lines?
11. Is an ant symmetrical?
12. What is $\frac{1}{2}$ of 32?
13. $\frac{6}{10}$ = 0.6, 6 or 60?
14. 900 – 220 =
15. 35p + 45p + £1.00 = £
16. 100 ÷ 10 =
17. 11 x 3 =
18. Is a square regular or irregular?
19. Draw two parallel lines.
20. James has 89 marbles. Luke has 76 marbles. How many fewer has Luke?

WEDNESDAY

1. 100 g + 250 g = _____ g
2. £5.00 − £1.40 =
3. 7 x 8 = 8 x
4. 3100 − 500 =
5. 13 − 9 =
6. 9 x 4 =
7. 3)‾27 =
8. Can this tessellate?
9. Sarah makes 95 biscuits. She sells 83. How many has she got left?
10. The meaning of the 4 in 400?
11. What is $\frac{1}{4}$ of 20?
12. Has a circle got parallel lines?
13. 900 − 420 =
14. Edges on a triangular prism?
15. 7 + 4 =
16. 25 x 2 =
17. Draw $\frac{1}{2}$ turn left.
18. Round 398 (nearest 10).
19. Share 28 drinks between 7 people. How many each?
20. Draw a vertical line.

THURSDAY

1. 400 g + 550 g = _____ g
2. 40 − 15 =
3. 0 x 4 = 4 x
4. 6 x 9 =
5. Monty the dog has 54 bones. He buries 14. How many has Monty got left?
6. Treble 7 =
7. Draw after a $\frac{3}{4}$ turn anticlockwise.
8. Sum of 10 and 12 =
9. 3 x 12 =
10. What is $\frac{3}{4}$ of 16?
11. Has a hexagon got parallel lines?
12. £1.10 + £0.90 =
13. 9)‾54 =
14. What month is 3.9.06?
15. 160 − 70 =
16. Share 32 pencils between 4 girls. How many each?
17. Draw a reflection.
18. 1.1, 1.2, 1.3, _____, 1.5
19. £2.00 − £0.45 =
20. 27 ÷ 9 =

New wave mental maths

MONDAY

1. 15 g – 12 g =   g
2. 20 – 5 =
3. £1.00 – 45p =
4. 7 ÷ 2 =   r
5. What is the chance of it raining today?
   ☐ impossible ☐ not sure ☐ possible
   ☐ might ☐ certain
6. 5 x 4 = (3 x 4) + (x 4)
7.   2 3
     x   2
8. $1/10$ = 0.1 ☐ true ☐ false
9. 4)‾20
10. 70 + 30 =
11. 500 mL add 250 mL =   mL
12. $\frac{1}{2}$ = $\frac{3}{4}$ ☐ true ☐ false
13. £2.50 =   p
14. Will a cube stack?
15. Which shape are the faces of a cube?

16. 8 x 9 =
17. Tick the right angle.
18. Circle the largest. **0.4 0.2 0.7**
19. ☐ A ⇨ ☐
    Draw $1/4$ turn left.
20. Write these fractions on the number line.
    $3/4$, $1/2$, $4/10$

    0 ————————————— 1

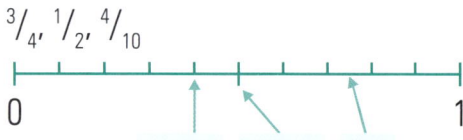

TUESDAY

1. 20 g – 5 g =   g
2. 5 ÷ 2 =   r
3. 30 – 15 =
4. Cost of buying 1 m of elastic at 40p per 50 cm?
5. £1.00 – 61p =
6. What 2 shapes make a square pyramid?
   _____ and _____
7. Is this an irregular shape?
8. Has the shape got parallel lines?
9. 5)‾35 =
10. $5/10$ = 0.5, 5, 50?
11.   4 1
      x 2
12. 250 mL + 250 mL =   mL
13. $\frac{1}{4}$ = $\frac{4}{8}$ ☐ true ☐ false
14. 14 – 7 =
15. 380 + 120 =
16. Which pet was the most popular?

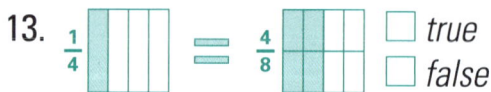

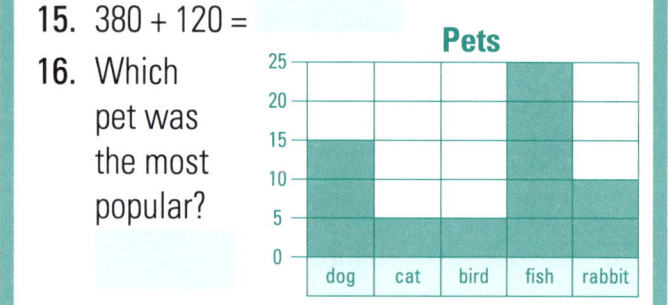

    Pets
    (bar chart: dog 15, cat 5, bird 25, fish 10, rabbit 10)

17. Which pet was there 10 of?
18. Which pets were the least popular?
    _____ and _____
19. How many dogs and rabbits?
20. How many animals altogether?

WEDNESDAY

1. 220 g − 20 g =   g
2. 7 ÷ 3 =   r
3. 14 + 18 =
4. Tick the right angles.
5. 7)̅2̅8̅ =
6. Edges on a cube?
7. Circle the smallest.
   0.3   0.6   0.2
8.   1 3
     x 2
9. 250 mL + 250 mL + 250 mL =   mL
10. 23 − 8 =
11. £3.25 =   p
12. Draw a vertical line.
13. Shaded area =   squares
14. 3 x 4 = (1 x 4) + (x 4)
15. $2/10$ = 0.2   ☐ true   ☐ false
16. Will a cone roll?
17. What shape?
18. 40 − 25 =
19. Draw an arrow going anticlockwise.
20. What is the chance of you wearing a pair of shoes to school?
    ☐ impossible   ☐ not sure   ☐ possible
    ☐ might   ☐ certain

THURSDAY

1. 800 g − 500 g =   g
2. 67 − 8 =
3. £5.00 − £2.40 =
4. Name this shape.
5. 9 ÷ 2 =   r
6. 6 x 5 = (4 x 5) + (x 5)
7. Write these fractions on the number line. $6/10$, $2/8$, $3/4$
8. 6 x 7 =
9. Cost of buying 3 m of skipping rope at £2.00 per 50 cm?
   £
10. £9.99 =   p
11. Which shape are the faces of a cuboid?
12.   4 3
      x 2
13. 500 mL − 250 mL =   mL
14. 900 − 500 =
15. Draw the line of symmetry.
16. Has the arrow above got parallel lines?
17. 17 + 19 =
18. Tick the right angle.
19. 5 x 9 =
20. 9)̅4̅5̅ =

Prim-Ed Publishing   www.prim-ed.com   **New wave mental maths**   63

MONDAY

1. 400 g add 250 g = ____ g
2. 3 x 9 =
3. 8 ÷ 3 = ____ r
4. 81 – 10 =
5. £3.75 – 80p =
6. 8 x 5 = (3 x 5) + (____ x 5)
7. Draw a reflection. 
8. Does a cone have right angles? 
9.   2 3
   x 3
10. Circle the smallest.
   0.3   0.8   0.6
11. 1 litre add 3 litres = ____ litres
12. 4 x 5 =
13. Name this shape. 
14. Date a week from 18 May?
15. Draw $\frac{1}{4}$ turn clockwise. 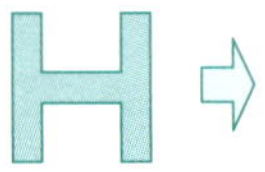
16. Has the H got parallel lines?
17. $\frac{8}{10}$ = 0.1, 0.8 or 8?
18. An irregular or regular hexagon? 
19. 12 x 9 =
20. 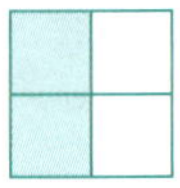 $\frac{1}{2}$ = $\frac{2}{4}$ ☐ true   ☐ false

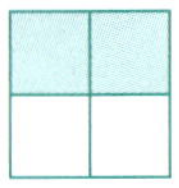

TUESDAY

1. 15 kg add 25 kg = ____ kg
2. 6 x 9 =
3. 6 ÷ 4 = ____ r
4. 15 + 45 = 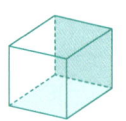
5. Does a cube have right angles?
6. £3.50 – 60p =
7. Cost of 4 kg flour at 50p per 500 g?
8. Draw a pair of parallel lines.
9. Name this 2-D shape. 
10. Difference between 50 and 8 =
11. 4 x 6 = (1 x 6) + (____ x 6)
12. Write zero point two as a numeral.
13.   1 2
   x 3
14. 0.6, 0.7, 0.8, ____
15. $\frac{3}{10}$ = 0.5   ☐ true   ☐ false
16. Write these fractions on the number line.
$\frac{1}{4}$, $\frac{9}{10}$, $\frac{4}{8}$ 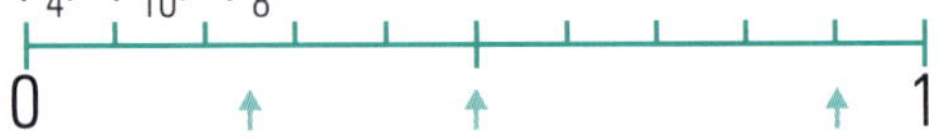
0 _____ 1
17. 15 litres add 20 litres = ____ litres
18. Write the number before 500.
19. 12 – 9 =
20. What is the chance of getting rotten teeth if you do not brush them?
☐ impossible ☐ not sure ☐ possible
☐ might ☐ certain

WEDNESDAY

1. 500 kg – 200 kg = ___ kg
2. 8 x 6 =
3. Name this 3-D shape.
4. Double 37.
5. 13 + 17 =
6. 9 ÷ 4 = ___ r
7. What day is the 11th?
8. How many days in the first week of January?
9. What day will 1st February be?
10. Write the dates of all the Sundays.
    ___ , ___ , ___ and ___
11. £4.20 – 35p =
12. 1, 4, 9, 16, 25, 36, ___
13. Does a cuboid have right angles?
14. 3 x 8 = (2 x 8) + (___ x 8)
15. Circle the smallest.
    0.5   0.9   0.2
16. 200 litres add 150 litres = ___ litres
17. £7.50 = ___ p
18. Can this tessellate?
19. Has the arrow above got horizontal lines?
20. Write a symmetrical number.

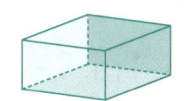

THURSDAY

1. 20 g subtract 18 g = ___ g
2. 7 x 8 =
3. Round 148 (nearest 10).
4. 8 ÷ 5 = ___ r
5. £2.30 – 35p =
6. Write these fractions on the number line. $\frac{6}{8}, \frac{3}{10}, \frac{1}{2}$
7. £1.00 – 25p =
8. 500 – 270 =
9. Halve 92.
10. 600 + 700 =

The chance of choosing the following shapes from the bag is:

11. Circle = ___ in 5.
12. Square = ___ in 5.
13. Triangle = ___ in 5.
14. 50 litres add 25 litres = ___ litres
15. What is the cost of 5 kg of watermelon at 20p per 500 g?
16.   2 1
    x 3
17. What is the chance of getting sunburnt in summer?
    ☐ impossible ☐ not sure ☐ possible
    ☐ might ☐ certain
18. $\frac{4}{10}$ = 0.4   ☐ true ☐ false
19. 17 – 8 =
20. 0.2, 0.4, 0.6, ___

MONDAY

1. 7 o'clock.  
2. 7 ÷ 4 =   r
3. Does a cylinder have right angles?
4. 5 x 9 = (2 x 9) + (x 9)
5.   2 0
   x 4
6. $^5/_{10}$ = 0.5 ☐ true ☐ false
7. 6 litres subtract 2 litres =   litres
8. £8.05 =   p
9. What shape is a tennis ball?
10. Draw a horizontal line.
11. £2.50 + £4.50 =
12. Circle the largest.   0.1   0.9   0.5
13. Can a cylinder stack?
14. 8 + 7 =
15. 40 ÷ 10 = 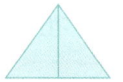
16. How many triangles can you find?
17. 7 x 4 =
18. Draw a reflection. 
19. Write these fractions on the number line.
$^3/_4$, $^2/_{10}$, $^4/_8$ 
0 ↑   ↑   ↑   1
20. 2)15 =   r

TUESDAY

1. 5 minutes past 8. 
2. 8 ÷ 5 =   r
3. 11 – 7 =
4. 3)16 =   r
5. 6 x 3 = (2 x 3) + (x 3)
6. £9.00 =   p
7. Name this shape. 
8. What shape is a telescope?
9. Sum of 8 and 9 =
10. Difference between 14 and 6.
11.   1 2
 x   4
12. Cost of 3 kg of cheese at £2.00 per 500 g =
13. Does a cuboid have right angles? 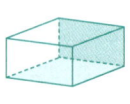
14. 50 litres – 30 litres =   litres
15. 2, 4, 6, 8, 10,
16. How many triangles? 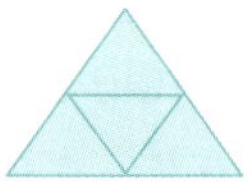
17. $^6/_8$  = $^3/_4$ ☐ true ☐ false
18. 2, 4, 8, 16,
19. Share 18 biscuits among 6 children. How many each?
20. How many gloves in 7 pairs?

WEDNESDAY

1. 25 minutes to 3. 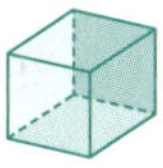
2. $9 \div 6 =$ ___ r
3. Does a cube have right angles?
4. Round 749 (nearest 100).
5. 45p + 55p =
6. $2\overline{)17}$ = ___ r
7. $5 \times 8 = (3 \times 8) + ($ ___ $\times 8)$
8. 45 litres – 20 litres = ___ litres
9. Draw 2 lines of symmetry. 
10. Has the 'H' got parallel lines?
11. £2.10 = ___ p
12. Draw ½ turn clockwise. 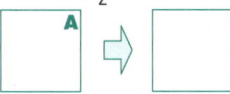
13. 0.4, 0.8, 1.2, ___
14. Edges on a cone? 
15. What type of weather was there most of?

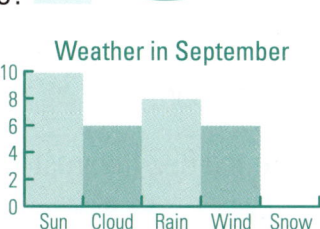

    Weather in September

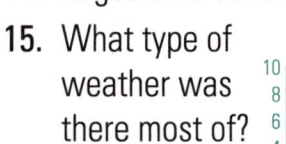

16. What type of weather was there none of?
17. Which season is this weather more likely to occur in?
18. How many rainy days were there?
19. Which two weather types occurred for the same amount of days? ___ and ___
20. How many days in September?

THURSDAY

1. Quarter to 7. 
2. $8 \div 7 =$ ___ r
3. Does a sphere have right angles? 
4. 10 – 6 =
5. Circle the smallest.   0.3   0.7   0.2
6. $9 \times 6 =$ 
7. Mark the right angle.
8. Has the triangle got a horizontal line?
9. 7 + 7 + 7 + 7 =
10.   1 1
     x   4
11. 75 litres – 50 litres = ___ litres
12. £7.50 = ___ p
13. $^6/_{10} = 0.3$ ☐ true ☐ false
14. Will a cuboid roll?
15. Double 16.
16. Name this shape. 
17. $3\overline{)20}$ = ___ r
18. 20p + 20p + 50p =
19. 400 – 150 =
20. What shape are dice?

MONDAY

1. 3:30
2. 6 × 5 =
3. 4)25 =   r
4. 7 × 6 = (3 × 6) + (× 6)
5. Cost of 1 kg jelly beans at 50p per 100 g = £
6. A 6-sided shape.

The chance of choosing the following shapes from the bag is:

7. Square =   in 7
8. Triangle =   in 7
9. Circle =   in 7
10. Rectangle =   in 7 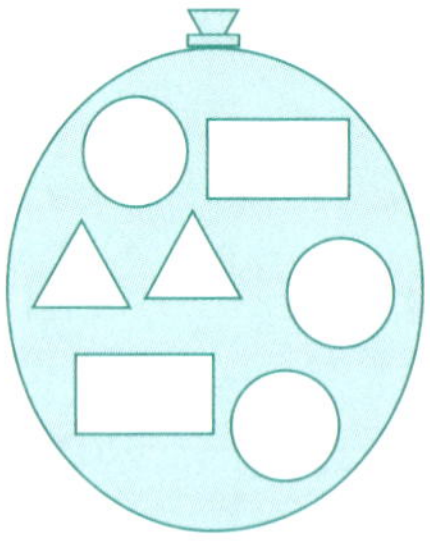
11. 9 + 7 =
12. 2 × 3 = 6, so 6 ÷ 3 =
13.   3 2
    ×   2

14. 25 cm add 74 cm =   cm
15. 14 − 10 =
16. $0.8 = \frac{4}{10}$ ☐ true ☐ false
17. Name this shape. 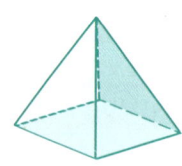
18. Write from largest to smallest.

0.8, 0.3, 0.5   ,   ,

19. 355p = £
20. Is this angle more or less than a right angle?

TUESDAY

1. 8:25 
2. Is this angle more or less than a right angle? 
3. 3 × 4 =
4. 100 cm + 40 cm =   m
5. 8 × 5 = 40, so 40 ÷ 5 =
6. Cost of 1 kg of almonds at £2.00 per 100 g =   £
7. 5)37 =   r
8. Name this shape. 
9. How many maths lessons in 1 week?

MONDAY	TUESDAY	WEDNESDAY	THURSDAY	FRIDAY
Maths	Maths	English	English	English
B	R	E	A	K
English	English	Maths	Maths	Maths
L	U	N	C	H
Science	P.E.	History	Art	RE
Science	Music	Drama	PSHE	Geography

10. Which lesson is after lunch on a Wednesday?
11. Which lesson is last on a Friday?
12. Which lesson are there 2 of each week?
13. Which 2 lessons are on a Tuesday afternoon?   and
14. Round 892 (nearest 100)
15. 950p = £
16. Which 2 shapes are the faces of a triangular prism?

      and

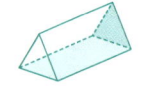

17. 4 + 9 =
18. Take 4 from 10.
19. 3 ÷ 3 =
20. What chance do you have of getting £1.00 for going to school?
    ☐ impossible ☐ not sure ☐ possible
    ☐ might   ☐ certain

68 — New wave mental maths — www.prim-ed.com — Prim-Ed Publishing

WEDNESDAY

1. 2:55
2. 12 − 9 =
3. 4)27 =   r
4. 500 − 190 =
5. 6 × 5 = (4 × 5) + (× 5)
6. Is M symmetrical?
7. Has the 'M' got vertical lines?
8. 50 + 90 =
9. 5 × 9 =
10. 704p = £
11. Cost of 1 m of liquorice at 10p per 10 cm.   £
12. 5 × 9 = 45, so 45 ÷ 9 =
13. Write from smallest to largest.
    0.1, 0.9, 0.3
    _____ , _____ , _____
14.   2 1
       × 4
15. Which 2 shapes are the faces of this pyramid? 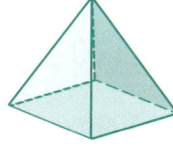
    _____ and _____
16. Double 19.
17. What 2 shapes make a cylinder?
    _____ and _____
18. 0.7 = $^7/_{10}$ ☐ true ☐ false
19. 65 cm + 35 cm =   cm
20. 50 + 50 + 50 =

THURSDAY

1. 4:40 
2. 7 + 4 =
3. Vertices in a square pyramid.
4. What chance is there of the sun shining today?
   ☐ impossible ☐ not sure ☐ possible
   ☐ might ☐ certain
5. 890p = £
6. Will this tessellate? 
7. Halve 14.
8. 17 − 9 =
9. Name this shape. 
10. Has the shape above got vertical lines?
11. 5)41 =   r
12. Buy 2 kg of sultanas at £1.00 per 500 g = £
13. Is this angle < more or less than a right angle?
14. 5 × 10 = (2 × 10) + (× 10)
15. 3 × 4 =
16. 210 cm + 70 cm =   cm
17. 6 + 5 =
18. How many right angles in a circle?
19. 3 × 10 = 30, so 30 ÷ 10 =
20. Write the fractions on the number line.
    $^7/_8$, $^1/_{10}$, $^1/_4$
    0 ↑   ↑ 1

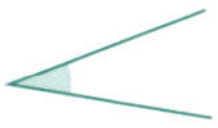

MONDAY

1. Time? _____ o'clock [12:00]
2. 6)19 = _____ r
3. If you rode your bike for 7 km in 30 minutes, how far in an hour? _____ km
4. Double 49.
5. 800 − 230 =
6. Is this angle _____ more or less than a right angle?
7. 	4 4
   x 2
8. 0.6, 0.8, _____, 1.2
9. 90 + 70 =
10. 8 x 4 = 32, so 32 ÷ 8 =
11. Write from smallest to largest.
    0.4, 0.7, 0.5
    _____, _____, _____
12. Colour $1/2$ the shapes.
13. 55 cm − 25 cm = _____ cm
14. 325p = £
15. Share 24 bones between 6 dogs. How many each?
16. Write the decimals on the number line.
    0.5, 0.2, 0.8
17. Draw a $1/2$ turn clockwise.
18. 0.9 = $9/10$ ☐ true ☐ false
19. How many socks in 10 pairs?
20. 8 x 4 =

TUESDAY

1. Time? _____ past [5:30]
2. Is this angle _____ more or less than a right angle?
3. 5 x 7 = 35, so 35 ÷ 5 =
4. 	2 3
   x 3
5. £4.70 − £1.20 =
6. Round 950 (nearest 100).
7. 7 ÷ 7 =
8. Colour $3/4$ of the shapes.
9. A B C D E F
   Tick the 3 shapes which have 2 sets of parallel lines.
10. How many toes on 4 feet?
11. How many triangles can you find?
12. 7)24 = _____ r
13. £1.00 − 39p =
14. 499p = £
15. 80 cm − 35 cm = _____ cm
16. 0.2 = $5/10$ ☐ true ☐ false
17. Take 6 from 12.
18. Draw a vertical line.
19. 7 x 8 =
20. Tick the most likely event:
    ☐ You will be asleep at midnight.
    ☐ You will turn into a pumpkin at midnight.

WEDNESDAY

1. Time?   to   11:55
2. 65 + 15 =
3. 170 − 80 =
4.   2 1
     x   4

5. Halve 94.
6. Name this shape. 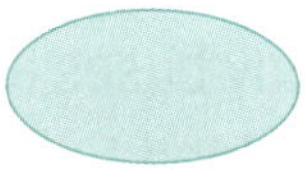
7. Has the above shape got vertical lines?
8. 140 cm − 60 cm =   cm
9. Measure this line.   cm 
10. 6)28 =   r
11. 72, 63, 54, 45,

The chance of pulling the following shapes from the bag is:

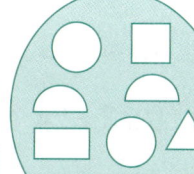

12. Circle =   in
13. Square =   in
14. Rectangle =   in
15. Semicircle =   in
16. Triangle =   in
17. 3 x 9 =
18. Name this shape. 
19. Write from smallest to largest.
    0.6, 0.4, 0.8
20. Colour $^6/_{10}$ of the shapes.

THURSDAY

1. Time?   past   8:15
2. 7)30 =   r
3. Colour $^7/_8$ of the shapes. 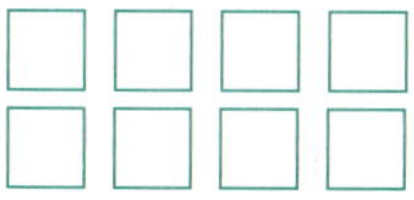
4. 200 cm − 150 cm =   cm
5. Draw a reflection. 
6. Name this shape. 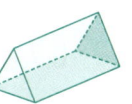
7. Is this angle    more or less than than a right angle?
8. 10 x 7 = 70, so 70 ÷ 10 =
9. 15 + 9 =
10. 60, 54, 48, 42,
11. Write the decimals on the number line.
    0.3, 0.7, 0.1

12. £0.65 + £0.35 =
13. 320p = £
14. 12 − 7 =
15. Tick the least likely event:
    ☐ A dog will talk to you on your way home.
    ☐ A dog will bark at you on your way home.
16. How many days in 3 full weeks?
17. Share 36 sweets between 6 people. How many each?
18. 5)26 =   r
19. 7 x 6 =
20. $\frac{6}{6}$ 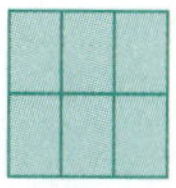 = $\frac{2}{6}$ ☐ true   ☐ false

Prim-Ed Publishing   www.prim-ed.com   **New wave mental maths**   71

MONDAY

1. Time? _____ to _____ [2:45]
2. What is the cost of 1 L of olive oil at £2.00 per 100 mL?
   £ _____
3. Round 149 (nearest 100).
4. Write from smallest to largest.
   0.7, 0.3, 0.2
   _____, _____, _____
5. 154p = £ _____
6. 8 + 8 + 8 + 8 =
7. $9\overline{)30}$ = _____ r _____
8.   3 4
     x 2
9. $\frac{1}{4}$ of 32 =
10. 8 x 4 = 32, so 32 ÷ 8 =
11. Draw a reflection.   b |
12. 35 + 45 =
13. £10.00 − £3.30 =
14. 50 m add 25 m = _____ m
15. 6 x 8 =
16. 0.3 = $^6/_{10}$ ☐ true ☐ false
17. Sum of 7 and 9 =
18. Difference between 120 and 80.
19. 900 − 320 =
20. Is this angle _____ more or less than a right angle?

TUESDAY

1. Time? _____ past _____ [5:10]
2. $\frac{1}{2}$ of 16 =
3. £500 − £140 =
4. Sum of 5 and 8 =

Bus timetable	Bus 1	Bus 2	Bus 3
Parkland	9.00 am	12.15 pm	4.30 pm
Somerton	9.20 am	12.35 pm	4.50 pm
Barksby	9.35 am	12.50 pm	5.05 pm
Denton	9.50 am	1.05 pm	5.20 pm
Carey	10.00 am	1.15 pm	5.30 pm

5. How many buses a day go from Parkland to Carey?
6. What time is the last bus from Somerton?
7. You need to be in Denton by 10 o'clock. What time do you need to catch a bus from Parkland?
8. How long does the bus take from Barksby to Denton?
9. What times do the buses arrive at Carey?
   _____, _____ and _____
10. 8 x 3 =
11. Write five hundred and nineteen as a numeral.
12. 19 − 10 =
13. 8 x 3 = 24, so 24 ÷ 3 =
14. $8\overline{)34}$ = _____ r _____
15. How many angles in a triangle?
16. Can this shape tessellate?
17. £2.20 + £1.80 =
18. Tick the most likely event.
    ☐ A frog will turn into a prince if you kiss it.
    ☐ A frog will croak if you kiss it.
19. Is this angle _____ more or less than a right angle?
20. Double 38.

WEDNESDAY

1. Time? ____ to ____ [10:35]
2. 7 + 7 =
3. Name this shape. ____

The chance of pulling the following coloured beads from the bag is:

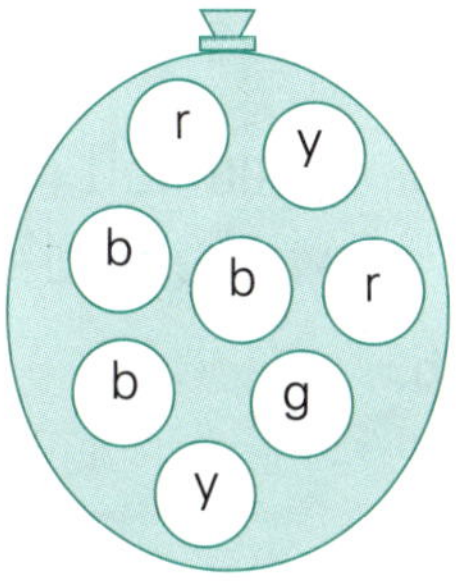

4. Blue = ____ in ____
5. Red = ____ in ____
6. Green = ____ in ____
7. Yellow = ____ in ____
8.   3 1
   x 3

9. $3/4$ of 12 =
10. 40 ÷ 10 =
11. ☐ regular shape
    ☐ irregular shape 
12. Tick which lines the above shape has:
    ☐ parallel ☐ vertical ☐ horizontal
13. 100 m add 250 m = ____ m
14. Is this symmetrical? ____ 
15. Is this angle  ____ more or less than a right angle?
16. 70 + 40 =
17. 8 x 10 = 80, so 80 ÷ 8 =
18. Draw a reflection. 
19. 9)44 = ____ r
20. 9 x 7 =

THURSDAY

1. Time? ____ past ____ [3:20]
2. 8)42 = ____ r
3. Difference between 100 and 70?
4. Name this shape. ____ 
5. £100.00 – £47.00 =
6. 9 x 3 = 27, so 27 ÷ 9 =
7. $0.5 = {}^5/_{10}$ ☐ true ☐ false
8. £1.00 – 71p =
9. 4 x 7 =
10. 122 – 22 =
11. Draw $3/4$ turn left. 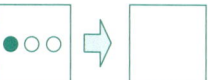
12. How many ears on 9 faces?
13. Share 90 worms between 10 birds. How many each?
14. 909p = £____
15. 500 m + 250 m = ____ m
16. $3/4$ of 20 =
17. Write from smallest to largest.
    0.3, 0.5, 0.1
    ____ , ____ , ____
18. Date a week before 16.7.06?
19. 12 + 19 =
20. Tick the least likely event:
    ☐ Tomorrow will be Friday.
    ☐ Tomorrow will be Saturday.

Prim-Ed Publishing   www.prim-ed.com   **New wave mental maths**   73

MONDAY

1. Quarter past 10 ☐:☐
2. 40 + 90 =
3. £2.50 + £2.50 =
4.
   ```
      4 0
   x     2
   ```
5. $^2/_{10}$ = 0.2 ☐ true ☐ false
6. $^2/_{10}$ of 100 =
7. 8 x 7 =
8. Is $^1/_4$ equivalent to $^2/_8$?
9. How many vertices on a cube? 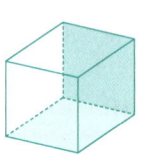
10. Tick which lines the cube has.
    ☐ parallel ☐ vertical ☐ horizontal
11. Draw a horizontal line.
12. 10)̅2̅2̅ =   r
13. $^1/_2$ of a number is six. What is the number?
14. 50 m subtract 30 m =   m
15. Edges on a cylinder.
16. 60 – 15 =
17. Surfaces on a sphere?
18. Which rectangle has more area? 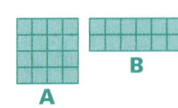
19. 8 x 8 = 64, so 64 ÷ 8 =
20. Is this angle more or less than a right angle?

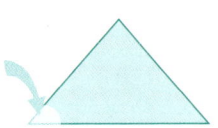

TUESDAY

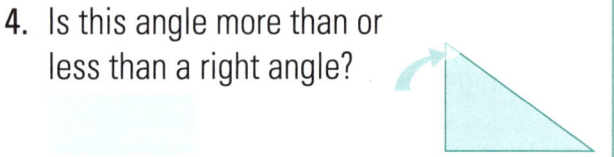

1. 5 o'clock ☐:☐
2. 10)̅5̅4̅ =   r 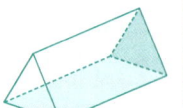
3. Name this shape.
4. Is this angle more than or less than a right angle?
5. Is your left shoe symmetrical? ☐ yes ☐ no
6.
   ```
      1 2
   x     4
   ```
7. 100 m – 70 m =   m
8. $^1/_4$ of a number is 4. What is the number?
9. What 3-D shape is a door?
10. 140 – 90 =
11. Kate has 52p. Jack has 34p. How much altogether?   p
12. 17 + 16 =
13. Write from largest to smallest. **0.3   0.9   0.2**
14. 4 x 9 =
15. Shade $^3/_{10}$. 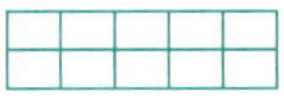
16. £4.50 + £1.50 =
17. 80 + 50 =
18. 9 x 2 = 18, so 18 ÷ 2 =
19. $^3/_8$ of 80 =
20. Which shape has more area?

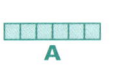

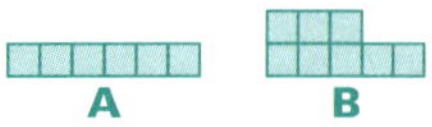

WEDNESDAY

1. Ten past 8. ☐:☐
2. 10)58 = ☐ r ☐
3. Sum of 50 and 90 =
4. 5 x 6 = 30, so 30 ÷ 6 =
5. Write from largest to smallest.   **0.5   0.1   0.7**
6. $\frac{1}{4}$ of 40 =
7. $\frac{3}{4}$ of a number is 9. What is the number?
8. 250 m – 150 m = ☐ m
9. 6 x 6 =
10. 400 + ☐ = 500
11. 900 – 500 =
12. Write these decimals on the number line.
    0.6   0.2   0.9
13. Jude has 26p. Kelly has 31p. Mark has 42p. How much altogether?
14. £6.50 + £3.50 =
15. Is $\frac{1}{2}$ equivalent to $\frac{5}{10}$?
16. 7 x 8 =
17. What shape do you see in the cross-section?
18. Round 326 (nearest 10).
19. How many socks in 7 pairs?
20. Is this angle more or less than a right angle?

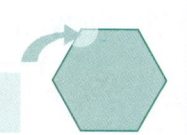

THURSDAY

1. Five to 11. ☐:☐
2. 8 + 2 =
3. 700 – 300 =
4. 8)65 = ☐ r ☐
5. 0.5 = $\frac{4}{10}$ ☐ true ☐ false
6. 16 – 7 =
7. Surfaces on a sphere?
8. 6 x 4 = 24, so 24 ÷ 4 =
9. Halve 52.
10. $\frac{1}{2}$ of a number is 10. What is the number?
11. 500 m – 400 m = ☐ m
12. Edges on a sphere?
13. How many toes on 6 feet?
14. 10 x 8 =
15. $\frac{3}{4}$ of 24 =

Favourite Harry Potter Characters

16. Who is the most popular character?
17. Who is the least popular character?
18. How many more people liked Hermione than Ron?
19. How many people chose Dobby?
20. How many people chose a favourite character?

MONDAY

1. Half past 2. ☐:☐
2. 0.6 = $^6/_{10}$ ☐ true ☐ false
3. 13 − 8 =
4. Name this shape. 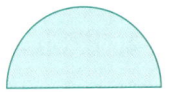
5. Write from largest to smallest.
   0.3, 0.9, 0.2
   ___ , ___ , ___
6. Surfaces on a cone?
7. Date is 3 July. What was the date a week before?
8. $\frac{1}{4}$ of a number is 8. What is the number?
9. Is this angle more or less than a right angle? 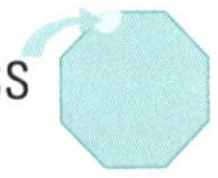
10. Sum of 65 and 25 =
11. What month is 3.4.06?
12. 13 − 8 =
13.   1 3
      x 3
14. Round 247 (nearest 10).
15. Arrange the digits into the highest value. 3, 0, 7
16. 7)46 = ___ r ___
17. 7 x 8 =
18. 5 x 6 = 30, 30 ÷ 5 =
    6 x 5 = ___ , 30 ÷ 6 =
19. Sam has 41p. Emma has 24p. How much altogether? ___ p
20. Can ◇ tessellate?

TUESDAY

1. Quarter to 4. ☐:☐
2. Number of edges on a cone =
3. 17 + 8 =
4. 2)19 = ___ r ___
5. Round 474 (nearest 10).
6. Is a wheel a sphere?
   The chance of pulling the following coloured beads from the bag is: 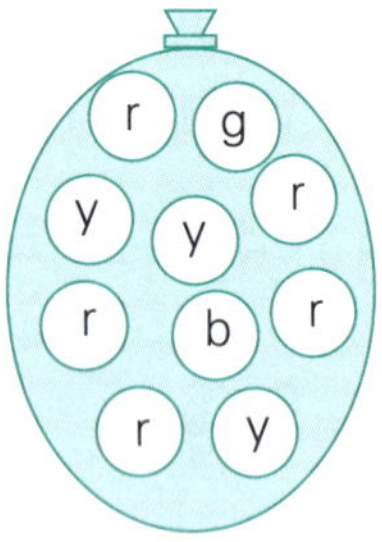
7. Green = ___ in ___
8. Blue = ___ in ___
9. Yellow = ___ in ___
10. Red = ___ in ___
11. Draw a reflection. 
12. 4 x 3 = 12, 12 ÷ 3 =
    3 x 4 = ___ , 12 ÷ 4 =
13. 520 + 180 =
14. 7 x 6 =
15. Name this shape. 
16. Tick the least likely event:
    ☐ Tomorrow you will be taller than your school.
    ☐ Tomorrow you will be the same height as today.
17. How many eyes on 8 heads?
18. $^3/_4$ of a number is 6. What is the number?
19. $^7/_{10}$ = 0.3 ☐ true ☐ false
20. Draw after a $^3/_4$ turn left.

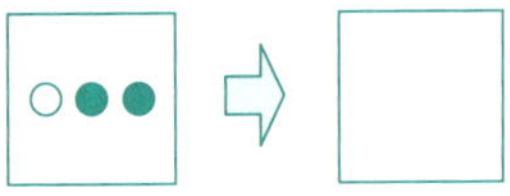

WEDNESDAY

1. Twenty past 11. ☐:☐
2. 0.5, 1, 1.5, ____ , 2.5
3. 7)31 = ____ r
4. 11 − 6 =
5.   3 4
    x 2
6. How many days in 5 full weeks?
7. £1.00 − 42p =
8. 600 + ____ = 900
9. What is the name of this shape?
10. Tick which lines the above shape has:
    ☐ parallel ☐ vertical ☐ horizontal
11. 110 − 70 =
12. 6 x 3 =
13. Tick the most likely event:
    ☐ A flower will die if you pick it.
    ☐ A flower will grow bigger if you pick it.
14. Share 14 apples between 7 children. How many each?
15. Double 28.
16. 10 x 3 = 30, 30 ÷ 10 =
    3 x 10 = ____ , 30 ÷ 3 =
17. Draw an oval.
18. In 792, what is the place value of the 9?
19. Write from largest to smallest.
    0.3, 0.9, 0.6
    ____ , ____ , ____
20. Is this angle more or less than a right angle?

THURSDAY

1. Twenty-five to 8. ☐:☐
2. £7.50 + £2.50 =
3. 3)29 = ____ r
4. 3 x 9 =
5. Draw a line of symmetry on this shape.
6. Tick which lines the above shape has:
    ☐ parallel ☐ vertical ☐ horizontal
7. 12 − 10 =
8. How many toes on 9 feet?
9. Share 30 pencils between 6 people. How many each?
10. 500 + ____ = 750
11. Surfaces on a cone?
12. 4 x 3 =
13. Which set of lines are parallel?
    A   B   C
14. 700 − 190 =
15. $\frac{1}{2}$ of a number is 20. What is the number?
16. Emily has 33p. George has 14p. Keira has 52p. How much altogether?
17. Write nine hundred and seventy as a numeral.
18. 18 + 14 =
19. 2 x 9 = 18, 18 ÷ 9 =
    9 x 2 = ____ , 18 ÷ 2 =
20. Which 2 shapes make a cylinder?
    ____ and ____

Prim-Ed Publishing   www.prim-ed.com   **New wave mental maths**   77

MONDAY

1. $1\frac{1}{4}$ hours = ____ hour(s) ____ minute(s)
2. Measure this line. ⊢—⊣
   ____ cm
3. Circle the answer.
   < right angle
   > right angle
   = right angle
4. Halve 38.
5. 3 x 7 = 21, 21 ÷ 7 =
   7 x 3 = ____ , 21 ÷ 3 =
6.   4 3
     x 2
7. 3)‾26 = ____ r
8. Surfaces on a solid sphere?
9. $\frac{3}{4}$ of a number is 15. What is the number?
10. 0.3 = $\frac{3}{10}$ ☐ true ☐ false
11. Surfaces on a solid cylinder?
12. Kevin has 59p. Sue has 45p. How much more has Kevin? ____ p
13. How many toes on 8 feet?
14. 7 x 9 =
15. 800 − ____ = 500
16. Draw after a $\frac{3}{4}$ turn right.
17. Which has more area? (shaded) A B
18. Write from smallest to largest. 0.2, 0.8, 0.1
    ____ , ____ , ____
19. 8 + 5 =
20. Tick the most likely event:
    ☐ You will do work at school today.
    ☐ You will go to sleep at school today.

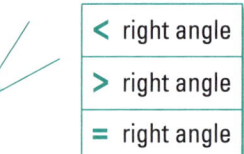

TUESDAY

1. $1\frac{3}{4}$ hours = ____ hour(s) ____ minute(s)
2. 8 + 9 =
3. How many socks in 7 pairs?
4. 350 + 450 =
   The chance of pulling the following shapes from the bag is:
5. Rectangle = ____ in
6. Square = ____ in
7. Oval = ____ in
8. Triangle = ____ in
9. Which 2 shapes have the least chance of being picked?
   ____ and ____
10. Which 2 shapes have the greatest chance of being picked?
    ____ and ____
11. 4 x 7 =
12. 8)‾60 = ____ r
13. 800 − 280 =
14. 12 − 6 =
15. 4 x 10 = 40, 40 ÷ 4 =
    10 x 4 = ____ , 40 ÷ 10 =
16. $\frac{8}{10}$ of a number is 80. What is the number?
17. Name this 2-D shape.
18. Is this a cylinder?
19. Draw a reflection.
20. Circle the answer.
    < right angle
    > right angle
    = right angle

WEDNESDAY

1. 2½ hours = _____ hour(s) _____ minute(s)
2. 4 x 8 =
3. 6)‾39 = _____ r
4. Write the decimals on the number line.
   0.7, 0.1, 0.5 

   0 ———————————— 1
5. 9 x 7 =
6. 10 x 3 =
7. Which is the analogue clock? A or B? 
   A ☐ B ☐
   9:45
8. Sum of 6 and 4 =
9. Draw a reflection. B
10. Tick which lines the letter 'B' has:
    ☐ parallel ☐ vertical ☐ horizontal
11. Circle the correct answer. 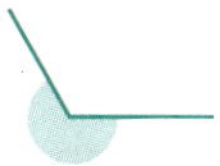
    < right angle
    > right angle
    = right angle
12. 11 + 10 + 9 + 8 =
13. Betty has 78p. John has 51p. How much less has John? _____ p
14. 13 – 5 =
15. Draw ¼ turn left. 
16. Share 45 cakes between 9 people. How many each?
17. 900 – _____ = 450
18. 5 x 4 =
19. Name this 3-D shape. 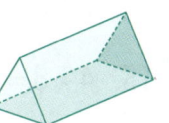
20. Circle the equivalent fractions.

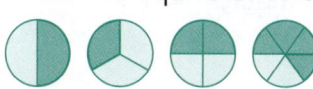

THURSDAY

1. 45 minutes = _____ hour(s) _____ minute(s)
2. 8 x 5 = 40, 40 ÷ 5 =
   5 x 8 = _____ , 40 ÷ 8 =
3. 8)‾60 = _____ r
4. Name this 3-D shape. 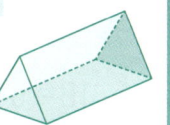
5. 500 – _____ = 350
6. 70 ÷ 10 =
7. ²⁄₁₀ = 0.5   ☐ true ☐ false
8. Write from largest to smallest.
   0.3, 0.8, 0.6
   _____ , _____ , _____
9. 6 x 8 =
10. ¹⁄₁₀ of a number is 2. What is the number?
11. 4, 8, 12. Rule =
12. 70 – 15 =
13. Tick which lines this shape has: 
    ☐ parallel ☐ vertical ☐ horizontal
14. Share 81p between 9 people. How much each? _____ p
15. 3 x 8 =
16. 900 – 110 =
17. Write the decimals on the number line.
    0.4, 0.7, 0.2 

    0 ———————————— 1
18. £0.85 + £0.25 =
19. 6)‾58 = _____ r
20. Tick the least likely event
    ☐ It will snow tomorrow.
    ☐ It will be sunny tomorrow.

MONDAY

1. Time?　　　　past 
2. 8 + 3 =
3. 10 ÷ 2 =
4. 15 − 5 =
5. 　　　3 3
　　　x　3

6. $^1/_{10}$ of a number is 5. What is the number?
7. Lucy has 97p. James has 45p. How much more has Lucy?　　p
8. 110 − 50 =
9. Name this shape. 
10. Draw a $^3/_4$ turn right. 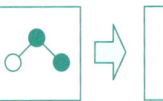
11. Cost of 1 kg of baby powder at 50p per 100 g = £
12. $^6/_{10}$ = 0.6　　☐ true ☐ false
13. 5)‾39 =　　r
14. Draw an arrow showing anticlockwise.
15. Circle the correct answer. 
   - < right angle
   - > right angle
   - = right angle
16. £5.00 − £3.90
   =
17. Name this shape. 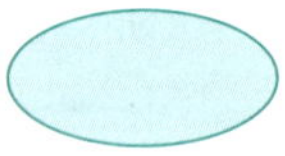
18. 6 x 7 = 42, 42 ÷ 6 =
   7 x 6 =　　, 42 ÷ 7 =
19. Write from largest to smallest.
   0.4, 0.9, 0.1

20. How many triangles can you find?

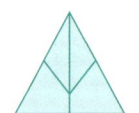

TUESDAY

1. Time?　　o'clock
2. 4)‾30 =　　r
3. Product of 9 and 4 =
4. 18 − 7 =

TV Guide		
Cartoons......6.00 am	News..........9.00 am	Film..........10.00 am
News..........6.30 am	Get fit!........9.15 am	Soap opera.11.30 am
GMTV..........7.00 am	Cartoons......9.45 am	News..........11.55 am

5. How many times is the news on?
6. How long is GMTV on for?
7. How many minutes are the cartoons on for altogether?
8. How much longer is 'Get Fit' on for than the soap opera?
9. What is on at quarter to ten?
10. Double 29.
11. How many gloves in 10 pairs?
12. Draw a reflection.　3
13. Circle the correct answer.
    - < right angle
    - > right angle
    - = right angle
14. £1.00 − 63p =
15. Steven has 86p. Sally has 25p. How much less has Sally?　p
16. 5 x 9 =
17. 33 + 17 =
18. 4 x 8 =　　, 32 ÷ 4 =
    8 x 4 =　　, 32 ÷ 8 =
19. $^4/_8$ of a number is 12. What is the number?
20. 7 x 8 =

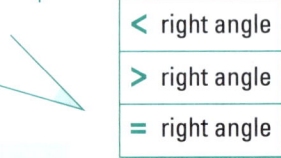

WEDNESDAY

1. Time? ____ past
2. 5)49 = ____ r
3.   4 2
   x   2

4. 10 x 5 = 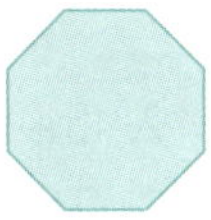
5. Tick which lines this shape has:
   ☐ parallel ☐ vertical ☐ horizontal

6. Difference between 12 and 6.
7. Circle the correct answer. 
   < right angle
   > right angle
   = right angle

8. 9 x 5 = 45, 45 ÷ 9 =
   5 x 9 = ____ , 45 ÷ 5 =

9. 12 + 11 + 8 =
10. Halve 72.

The chance of pulling the following coloured beads from the bag is:

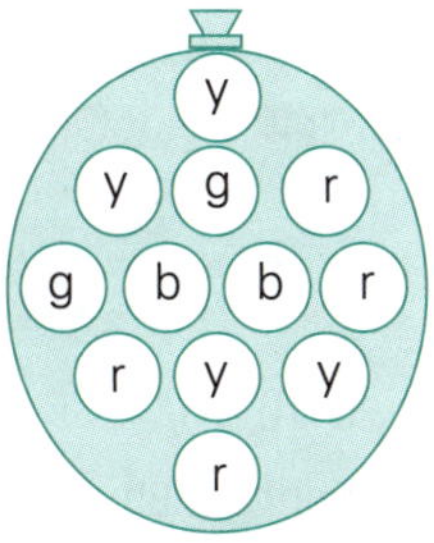

11. Yellow = ____ in
12. Green = ____ in
13. Red = ____ in
14. Blue = ____ in
15. Which 2 colours have the greatest chance of being picked?
    ____ and ____
16. Which two colours have the least chance of being picked?
    ____ and ____
17. $2/8$ of a number is 10. What is the number?
18. Name this shape.
19. Should a fence be vertical or horizontal? 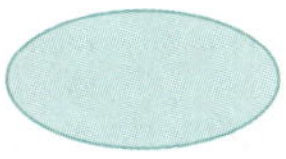
20. 26 + 24 =

THURSDAY

1. Time? ____ to
2. Can 290 be divided by 10 equally?
3. 9 x 3 =
4. 900 – 150 =
5. 25 + 45 =
6. 8 x 0 =
7.   2 1
   x   4

8. 12 + 19 =
9. Circle the correct answer.
   < right angle
   > right angle
   = right angle

10. 4 x 5 = 20, 20 ÷ 5 =
    5 x 4 = ____ , 20 ÷ 4 =

11. $8/10$ = 0.4 ☐ true ☐ false
12. 6 x 7 =
13. Name this shape. 
14. 8)60 = ____ r
15. 21 ÷ 3 =
16. $6/8$ of a number is 18. What is the number?
17. Draw a $1/4$ turn left.
18. Sum of 10 and 10 =
19. Write from smallest to largest.
    0.7, 0.2, 0.4
    ____ , ____ , ____
20. Draw the reflection.

FRIDAY TEST Week 1

1.  Time? ___ . ___ or ___ past 6.
2. 2 + 2 + 2 + 2 =
3. Write nineteen as a numeral.
4. 2, 4, 6, 8, ___, 12
5. Share 8 stars between 2 people. ___ stars each
6. How many days in a year?
7. 1 m = ___ cm
8.  ⚬⚬ + ⚬⚬ + ⚬⚬ =
9. 10 − 2 − 2 − 2 − 2 =
10. Is 10 odd or even?
11. Name this 2-D shape.
12. Share 8 ice-creams between 2 children. ___ each
13. 10 + 7 =
14. Is 7 odd or even?
15. Double 7.
16. Draw a semicircle in the box.
17. 10 − 6 =
18. How many days in a fortnight?
19. Tick which you would use to measure the classroom. ☐ cm ☐ m
20. 8 − 3 =
21. 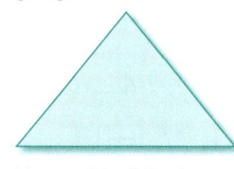 Name this 2-D shape.
22. 1 day = ___ hours
23. 500 + 20 + 5 =
24. Halve 16.
25. 40 + 20 =

FRIDAY TEST Week 2

1.  Time? ___ . ___ or ___ past 11.
2. 5 + 5 + 5 + 5 =
3. Take 10 eggs from one dozen. How many left?
4. Share 10 sweets between 5 people. ___ sweets each
5. Days in a leap year?
6. Would you drink a litre or a metre of water?
7. 5, 10, 15, ___, 25
8. Spring, Summer, ___ and Winter are the four seasons.
9. 20 − 5 − 5 =
10. 7 pairs of shoes = ___ shoes
11. 4 + 6 =
12. 34 − 10 =
13. How many days in a week?
14. 7 + 6 =
15. A hexagon = ___ sides
16. Is 15 odd or even?
17. 5 + 5 + 5 + 5 + 5 + 5 =
18. ___ minutes = 1 hour
19. Double 9.
20. A hexagon = ___ sides
21. Write one hundred and forty-seven as a numeral.
22. Name this 2-D shape.
23. Halve 50.
24. 9 − 3 =
25. 30 − 5 − 5 − 5 =

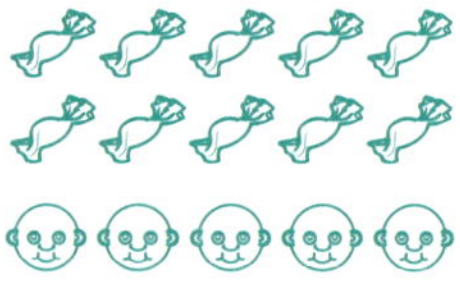

FRIDAY TEST Week 3

1. 12:20 _____ past
2. 10 + 10 + 10 = _____
3. Is Wednesday ☐ before ☐ after Tuesday?
4. In 374, what is the meaning of the 7? ☐ 700 ☐ 70 ☐ 7
5. 10, 20, _____, 40, 50
6. 30 + 40 = _____
7. 1, 3, _____, 7, 9, 11
8. A hexagon has _____ sides.
9. Write two hundred and eighty-three as a numeral. _____
10. Share 30 biscuits between 10 people. How many each? _____ biscuits each
11. 100 cm = _____ m
12. What day was yesterday? _____
13. 60 − 10 − 10 = _____
14. Draw a triangle in the box.
15. 43 + 10 = _____
16. Tick which you would use to measure a mouse. ☐ cm ☐ m
17. What is the meaning of 2 in 29? ☐ 20 ☐ 2
18.  Name this 3-D shape. _____
19. 8 + 4 = _____
20. 9 − 7 = _____
21. 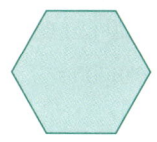 Name this 2-D shape. _____
22. What day is tomorrow? _____
23. 700 − 200 = _____
24. Double 10. _____
25. 14 − 4 = _____

FRIDAY TEST Week 4

1. 10:05 _____ past
2. 3 + 3 + 3 + 3 = _____
3. 15 − 3 − 3 = _____
4.  Name this 2-D shape. _____
5. What day was yesterday? _____
6. 3 + 4 = _____
7. 3, 6, 9, 12, _____, 18
8. 1, 3, _____, 7, 9, _____, 13, 15
9. Share 12 bananas between 3 people. How many each? _____ each
10. What month was last month? _____
11. 18 + 2 = _____
12. What day is tomorrow? _____
13. Semicircle = _____ sides
14.  Measure. _____ cm
15. Round 63 to the nearest ten. _____
16. 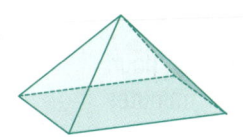 Name this 3-D shape. p
17. 24 − 10 = _____
18. £1.50 + £3.00 = _____
19. 2, _____, 6, 8, _____, 12, 14
20. How much for 9 lollies at 5p each? _____
21. 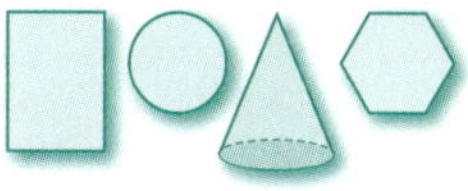 Tick the hexagon.
22. Rectangle = _____ corners
23. £1.00 − 40p = _____
24. 19 − 9 = _____
25. In 830, what is the place value of the 3? ☐ 100s ☐ 10s ☐ units

FRIDAY TEST Week 5

1. $\frac{1}{4}$ hour = _____ minutes
2. 2, 4, 6, ____, 10, 12
3. 4 + 4 + 4 + 4 =
4. Write two hundred and seventy-two as a number.
5. Which comes first?
   ☐ Christmas
   ☐ Easter
6. Round 86 to the nearest ten.
7. 4, 8, ____, 16, 20
8. Tick which you would use to measure a pathway.
   ☐ cm   ☐ m
9. 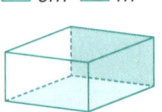 Name this 3-D shape.
   c_____ oi_____
10. £5.00 – £2.50 =
11. Share 16 balloons between 4 people. How many each?
    _____ balloons each
12. 200 + 700 =
13. How many blocks needed to fill the gaps? 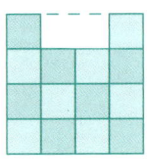
    _____ blocks
14. 7 + 8 =
15. Tick which happened a long time ago.
    ☐ You were 2.
    ☐ You were 16.
16. 11, 13, ____, 17
    Rule: add
17.  ⊢―⊣
    How long? _____ cm
18. A hexagon has _____ sides.
19.  ⟵⟶
    Vertical or horizontal?
20. 16 – 8 =
21. Name a 2-D, six-sided shape.
22. 3, 6, 9, 12, 15, ____
23. 20 – 4 – 4 =
24. Buy 4 books at £7.00 each.
    £ _____
25. 13 – 5 =

FRIDAY TEST Week 6

1. $\frac{3}{4}$ hour = _____ minutes
2. 3 + 9 =
3. Round 54 to the nearest ten.
4. 16 – 4 – 4 =
5. Share 20p between 4 children.
   _____ p each.
6. Which comes first?
   ☐ July   ☐ March
7. In 423, what is the meaning of the 4?
   ☐ 400 ☐ 40 ☐ 4
8. A hexagon = _____ sides
9. 12, 9, 6, 3.
   Rule: Subtract
10. 10, 20, 30, ____, 50
11. 20 wheels. How many cars?
12. Halve 24.
13. £6.00 + £2.50 =
14. 5, 8, 11, ____
15. 3 + 3 + 3 + 3 =
16. Share £30.00 between 3 people.
    £ _____ each
17. 9 + 5 =
18. Round 75 to the nearest ten.
19. What day is tomorrow?
20.  ☐ Clockwise or
    ☐ anticlockwise?
21. Would you buy sugar by the kilogram (kg) or the kilometre (km)?
22. Double 15.
23. A triangle = _____ corners
24. 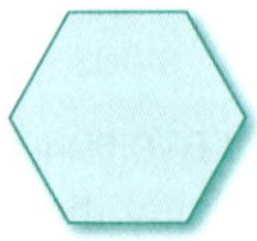 Name this 2-D shape.
25. 10 – 4 =

FRIDAY TEST Week 7

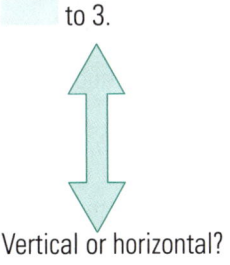

1.  Time? ___ . ___ or ___ to 3.
2. Vertical or horizontal?
3. A square is a ___-sided shape.
4. Draw an anticlockwise direction.
5. Cuboid = ___ faces.
6.  Name this 3-D shape.
7. Tick which you would use to measure a flower.
   ☐ cm ☐ m
8. 8 + 2 =
9. What time does school start?
10. 9 + ___ = 12
11.  Clockwise or anticlockwise?
12. 8 + 8 =
13. What is the number before 200?
14. A 6-sided shape is a ___.
15. 15 − 9 =
16. 5 x 2 =
17. Double 6.
18. Round 17 to the nearest ten.
19. In a 50 m pool, you swam 200 m. How many laps did you swim?
20. 12 ÷ 2 =
21. 9 x 2 =
22. Buy 3 boxes of chocolates at £3.00 each.
    Cost = £
23. Which comes first?
    ☐ May
    ☐ December
24. £5.00 − £1.50 =
25. 5, 9, 13, ___

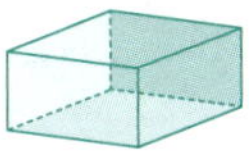

FRIDAY TEST Week 8

1.  Time? ___ . ___ or ___ to 3.
2. 134 cm = ___ m ___ cm
3. Which comes first?
   ☐ Boxing Day
   ☐ Christmas Day
4. Which is longer?
   ☐ 1 m
   ☐ 10 cm
5. 11 − 5 =
6. 4 x 5 =
7.  Name this 3-D shape.
8. 400 + 70 + 6 =
9. Round 95 to the nearest ten.
10. 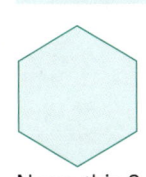 Name this 2-D shape.
11. What time does break start?
12. 11, ___, 15, 17, 19
13. Write three hundred and fifty-one as a numeral.
14. 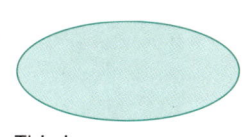 This is:
    ☐ a hexagon.
    ☐ an oval.
    ☐ a semicircle.
15. In 845, what is the meaning of the 8?
    ☐ 800 ☐ 80 ☐ 8
16. 600 + 300 =
17. 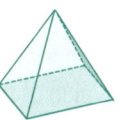 Name this shape.
    p ___ r ___ i ___
18. At 2 p.m., is it morning or afternoon?
19. £10.00 − £2.50 =
20. 30 ÷ 5 =
21. Share 5 chocolate bars among 5 children.
    ___ each
22. 8 + 7 =
23. 7 x 5 =
24.  Clockwise or anticlockwise?
25. Halve 30.

FRIDAY TEST Week 9

1. `3:50` to
2. Name this 3-D shape.
3.  How long? ___ cm
4. Round 24 to the nearest ten.
5. In 382, what is the place value of the 3?
   ☐ 100s ☐ 10s ☐ units
6. 80 + 90 =
7. 14 + ___ = 20
8. What time does lunch break start?
9. A square is a ___-sided shape.
10. Which comes first?
    ☐ morning
    ☐ evening
11. 255 cm = ___ m ___ cm
12. 59 − 10 =
13. 16, 14, 12, 10
    Rule: subtract ___
14. A triangle has ___ sides.
15. 600 + 300 =
16. 11, 13, 15, ___, 19
17. 15 − 9 =
18. £10.00 − £3.50 =
19. Share £35.00 among 5 teachers.
    £ ___ each
20. A hexagon is a ___-sided shape.
21. 60 ÷ 10 =
22. Cuboid = ___ corners
23. 900 − 700 =
24. Would you buy paint in metres or litres?
25.  Name this 2-D shape.

FRIDAY TEST Week 10

1. `11:35` to
2. 10 x 2 =
3. What time does school start?
4. What time does break finish?
5. Triangular prism = ___ corners
6. A hexagon is a 2-D shape with ___ sides.
7. Write five hundred and twenty-nine as a numeral.
8. Round 127 to the nearest ten.
9. 1 x 5 =
10. 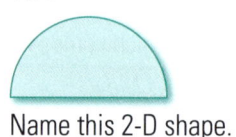 Name this 2-D shape.
11. 12 ÷ 2 =
12. Would you eat a kilogram or a kilometre of apples?
13. 553 cm = ___ m ___ cm
14.  Is this a semicircle?
15. 24, 20, 16
    Rule: subtract ___
16. 200 + 700 =
17. 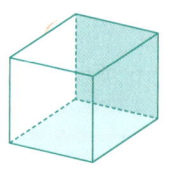 Name this 3-D shape.
18. 8 + 6 =
19. 14 − 9 =
20.  ☐ Clockwise or
    ☐ anticlockwise?
21. £5.00 + £8.50 = £ ___
22. 9 x 10 =
23. 5 ÷ 5 =
24. 60 ÷ 10 =
25.  Vertical or horizontal?

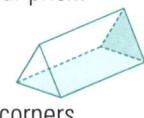

FRIDAY TEST Week 11

1. `8:50` ___ to ___
2. 4 + 9 =
3. Draw anticlockwise.

4. 5 x 3 =
5. 13 − 7 =
6. Draw a line of symmetry.

7. 6 x 3 =
8. 19 − 8 =
9. 1 L = ___ mL
10. 90 minutes =
    ___ hour(s)
    ___ minute(s)
11. Round 79 to the nearest 10.
12. 18.8.05
    What month is it?
13. Is P symmetrical?
14. 3 ÷ 3 =
15. Halve 16.
16. £1.95 = ___ p
17. 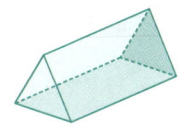 Name this 3-D shape.
18. 15 ÷ 3 =
19. Sum of 5 and 6 =
20. 4 + 4 + 4 + 4 =
21. What is the meaning of the 3 in 387?
22. What comes next?
23. 350 + 150 = 
24. On a 15-km bike ride, you have 5 km left. How many kilometres have you covered?
    ___ km
25. Measure this line.
    ___ cm 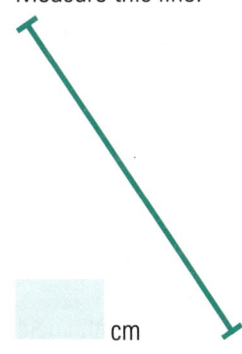

FRIDAY TEST Week 12

1. Quarter past 7. 
2. Double 7.
3. 12 − 9 =
4. 350 + 250 =
5. Tick which shape will stack. 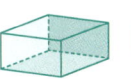
6. Divide £100 between 10 children.
    £ ___ each
7. 4 x 4 =
8. 20 ÷ 4 =
9. £4.25 = ___ p
10. The date is Monday, 4 August. What day will the 7th be?
11. 18 − ___ = 11
12. 12 metres add 8 metres =
    ___ metres
13. 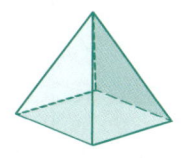 Name this 3-D shape.
    s___
    p___
14. 120 minutes =
    ___ hour(s)
    ___ minute(s)
15. Should an oak tree grow vertically or horizontally?
16. 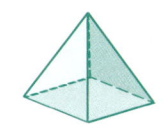 How many faces on a square pyramid?
17. 6 x 4 =
18. 4, 7, 10, 13, ___
19. £2.50 + £3.50 =
20. 500 − 150 =
21.  Name this 3-D shape.
22. Write two hundred and forty-five as a numeral.
23. What comes next? 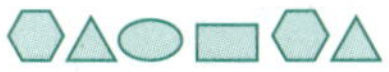
24. Sum of 9 and 8 =
25. 24 ÷ 4 =

FRIDAY TEST Week 13

1. 10 minutes to 4.

2. Is your teacher
   ☐ lighter
   ☐ heavier
   than 1 kg?

3. 6 + 6 + 6 =

4. 55 + 15 =

5. Share 12 sweets between 6 children. How many each?

   _____ sweets each

6. 10 litres of sticky glue at £6.00 per litre

   = £ _____

7. 17 − 9 =

8. How many faces on a cube?

9. 1 kg = _____ g

10. 150 + 550 =

11. In 398, what is the meaning of the 9?

12. 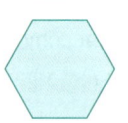 Name this 2-D shape.

13. Round 849 to the nearest 100.

14. 6, 12, 18, _____, 30, 36

15. 125 minutes =

    _____ hour(s)

    _____ minute(s)

16. Colour ³⁄₄

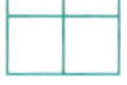

17. What comes after 519?

18. What is the chance of it raining today?
    ☐ possible
    ☐ impossible

19. 30 − 6 − 6 =

20. Is F symmetrical?

21. 15 metres add 6 metres =

    _____ metres

22. 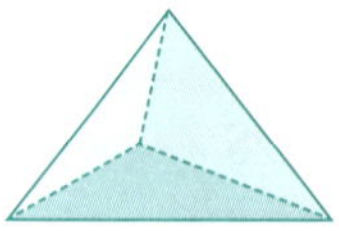 How many faces on this triangular pyramid?

23. 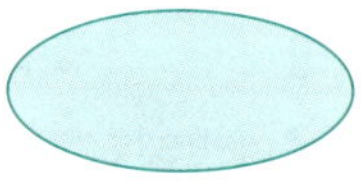 Name this 2-D shape.

24. 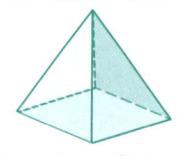 Name this 3-D shape.

25. How many faces does this shape have?

FRIDAY TEST Week 14

1. 20 minutes past 9.

2. Sum of 6 and 7 =

3. 1 × 6 =

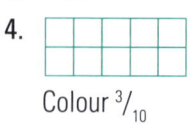

4. Colour ³⁄₁₀

5. What comes after 301?

6. The date is Wednesday, 18 December. What day will 23 December be?

7. £4.50 + £2.50 =

   £ _____

8. 25 − _____ = 18

9. Which is heavier, 1 g or 1 kg?

10. How many faces on a cube?

11. 140 minutes =

    _____ hour(s)

    _____ minute(s)

12. A hexagon = _____ -sided shape

13. Is Q symmetrical?

14. 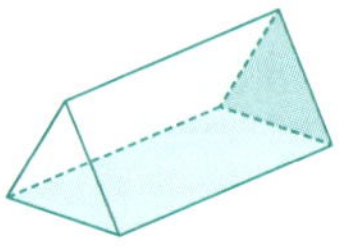 How many faces on a triangular prism?

15. Will this shape tessellate?

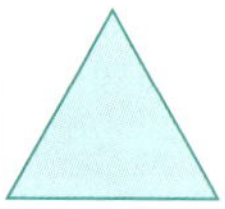

16. Colour ⁵⁄₈

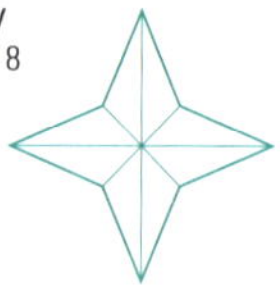

17. Plot the data on the graph.

    Favourite drinks
    Milk   4
    Juice   5
    Fizzy pop 3
    Squash   2

18. 1 m = _____ cm

19. £7.49 = _____ p

20. 8 + 8 + 8 =

21. 12 − 4 =

22. 18 ÷ 6 =

23. 5 × 6 =

24. In 338, what is the meaning of the numeral 8?

25. Halve 70.

FRIDAY TEST Week 15

1. Half past 8
2. 10 x 3 =
3. 17 − 8 =
4. Difference between 11 and 8 =
5. What comes next? 
6. 5 x 4 =
7.  Name this 3-D shape. (square pyramid)
8. How many faces on a triangular prism?
9. What comes after 869?
10. 6 + 6 + 6 + 6 =
11. What is the date one week before 19 November?
12. 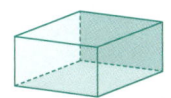 Name this 3-D shape.
13. 30 ÷ 6 =
14. Write eight hundred and eight as a numeral.
15. £1.00 − 55p =
16. 1 L = ___ mL
17. 624 + 153
18. Write as a fraction. 
19. What is the chance of you watching television this weekend?
    ☐ impossible
    ☐ possible
    ☐ certain
20. 4 m = ___ cm
21. 15 metres add 25 metres = ___ metres
22. 3, 6, 9,
23. Round 520 (nearest 100).
24. Colour $^7/_{10}$ 
25. How long would this line be?
    (a) 5 m (b) 5 cm

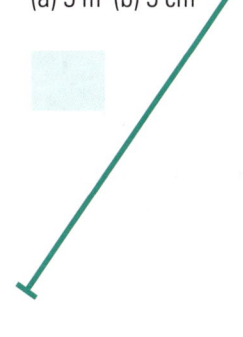

FRIDAY TEST Week 16

1. 5 minutes past 9.
2. 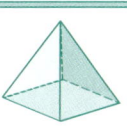 How many faces on this square pyramid?
3. Is 8 symmetrical?
4. 53, 52, 51,
5. 50 + 35 =
6. 1 kg = ___ g
7. How many faces on a triangular pyramid?
8. What is the meaning of the 2 in 283?
9. 24 + 5 = 29, so 34 + 5 =
10. £1.00 − 35p =
11.  Write as a fraction.
12. Round 352 to the nearest 100.
13. 4 x 0 =
14. Total cost of buying 5 m of ribbon at £3.00 per metre.
    = £
15. 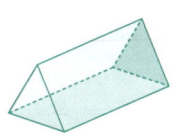 Name this 3-D shape.
16. 7, 14, ___, 28, 35
17. What is the chance of it being cloudy today?
    ☐ impossible
    ☐ possible
    ☐ certain
18. Would you measure apples in kilograms or litres?
19. How many triangles can you find? 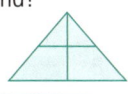
20. £5.25 = ___ p
21. Is $^1/_4$ the same as a $^1/_2$?
22. Share 35 apples between 7 children. How many each?
23. 3 + 8 + 5 =
24. 1 m = ___ cm
25. 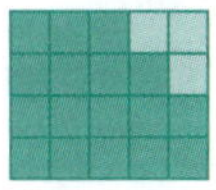 Shaded area = ___ squares

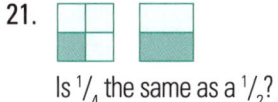

FRIDAY TEST Week 17

1. 20 minutes to 4.
   [:]
2. What month is 17.3.06?
3. 200 + ___ = 800
4. The date is Friday, 9 July. What day will 13 July be?
5. £7.95 = ___ p
6. 3 m = ___ cm
7. 1¼ hours = ___ hour(s) ___ minute(s)
8. 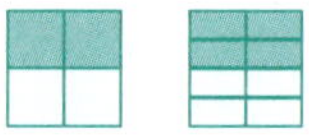 Is ²⁄₄ the same as ⁴⁄₈?
9. 9 + 6 =
10. 7 x 7 =
11. 15 + 75 =
12. What is the chance of your class getting an award from your teacher today?
    ☐ impossible
    ☐ possible
    ☐ certain
13. What is the difference between 17 and 9?
14. 35 ÷ 7 =
15. What number comes after 200?
16. Draw a vertical line.
17. How many faces? 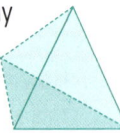
18. Write eight hundred and eighteen as a numeral.
19. How many surfaces on a solid cylinder?
20. Will this shape tessellate?
21. Write the fraction of the shaded area. 
22. 90 + 70 =
23. 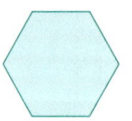 Name this 2-D shape.
24. 8 x 7 =
25. 3, 9, 15, 21, ___

FRIDAY TEST Week 18

1. 20 minutes past 11.
   [:]
2. 8 + 6 =
3. 80 + 70 =
4. Share 80 marshmallows between 8 people. How many each?
5. 8, 16, 24, ___, 40, 48
6. 100 + ___ = 900
7. What is the difference between £1.00 and 85p?
8. 650 + 150 =
9. 2½ hours = ___ hour(s) ___ minute(s)
10. 1 m = ___ cm
11. Round 760 to the nearest 100.
12. Using all of these digits, make the smallest number.
    2   8   1
13. What is the chance of you running faster than your teacher?
    ☐ impossible
    ☐ possible
    ☐ certain
14. 3 + 5 =
15. 900 – 350 =
16. 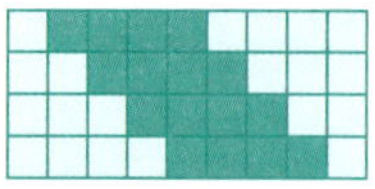 Shaded area = ___ squares
17. 20 cm add 9 cm = ___ cm
18. Is this a regular or irregular shape?
19. Write five hundred and ninety as a numeral.
20. Will a cube stack?
21. £3.05 = ___ p
22. How many faces on a cube?
23. What number comes after 699?
24. 9, 14, 19, 24, ___
25. 8 + 8 + 8 + 8 =

FRIDAY TEST Week 19

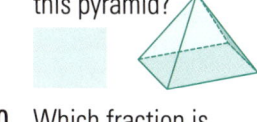

1. 1½ hours =
   _____ hour(s)
   _____ minute(s)
2. Select and shade ¾.
3. Share 20 footballs between 4 schools.
   _____ footballs per school.
4. 200 + _____ = 500
5. 48 ÷ 8 =
6. What is the chance of you reading a book this week?
   ☐ impossible
   ☐ possible
   ☐ certain
7. What is the difference between 19 and 8?
8. 8 m = _____ cm
9. 5 x 0 =
10. Measure this line. 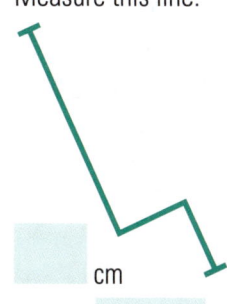
    _____ cm
11. £3.30 = _____ p
12. 4 x 8 =
13. 140 – 70 =
14. How many surfaces on a cone?
15. £5.00 – £2.50 =
16. Draw the line of symmetry. 
17. 170 – 90 =
18. 25 cm add 2 cm = _____ cm
19. How many faces on this pyramid?
20. Which fraction is smallest?
    ☐ ½   ☐ ¼
21. Plot the data on the graph.
    Favourite animals
    Dog   4
    Bird   3
    Seal   2
    Cat   3 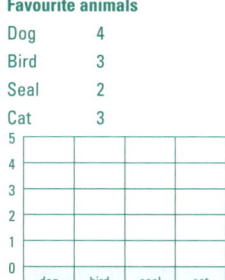
22. 800 – 350 =
23. Will a cube roll?
24. 9 x 8 =
25. How many triangles can you find?

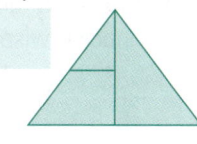

FRIDAY TEST Week 20

1. 2¾ hours =
   _____ hour(s)
   _____ minute(s)
2. What is the meaning of 9 in 89?
3. Round 95 (nearest 100).
4. 1 L = _____ mL
5. 9, 18, 27, _____, 45, 54
6. Shaded area = _____ squares
7. How many faces on a triangular prism?
8. 9 + 9 + 9 + 9 =
9. What is the chance of a phone ringing in your classroom?
   ☐ impossible
   ☐ possible
   ☐ certain
10. 6 x 0 =
11. 400 + _____ = 800
12. 120 – 80 =
13. Double 19.
14. 24 cm add 6 cm = _____ cm
15. How many faces on a triangular pyramid?
16. Complete this sequence. 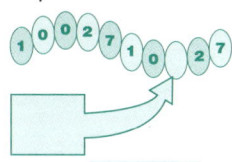
    100 27 10 27
17. £4.20 = _____ p
18. 12 + 12 + 12 =
19. 423
    +205
    ____
20. 36 – 9 – 9 =
21. How many vertices (corners) on a cuboid?
22. Which bucket holds more water?
    (a) ☐ 500 mL
    (b) ☐ 8 L
    (c) ☐ 1000 mL
23. £1.00 – 35p =
24. 8 + 4 + 7 =
25. 33 + 5 = 38, so 43 + 5 = _____

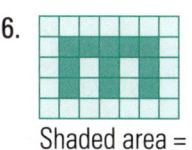

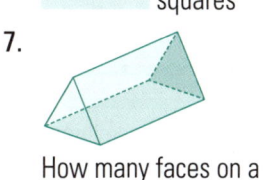

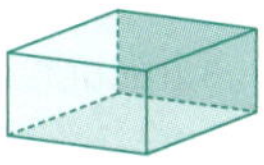

FRIDAY TEST Week 21

1. 24 cm + 12 cm = ___ cm
2. 8 + 9 =
3. 71 − 9 =
4. 18 ÷ 9 =
5. 420p = £
6. 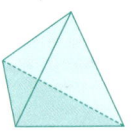 Name this 3-D shape.
7. Tick which contains the most.
   ☐ 1 litre jug
   ☐ 250 mL jug
8. Which fraction is the smallest?
   ☐ $4/8$ ☐ $3/4$
9. 7 x 9 =
10. 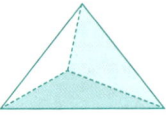 How many edges?
11. 0, 5, 15, 30, 50,
12. Which shape are the faces on a cuboid?
13. 110 − 30 =
14. Linda walked 3 km in 30 minutes. How far did Linda walk in one hour? ___ km
15. Tick the most likely event.
    ☐ You will shrink to the size of a matchstick.
    ☐ You will grow into an adult.
16. Draw $1/4$ turn right (clockwise).
17. What shape is a toilet roll? 
18. What is the chance of you washing your hands this week?
    ☐ impossible
    ☐ possible
    ☐ certain
19. 3, 6, 9, 12
    Rule: add
20.  Are these lines parallel?
21. What 2-D shape has 6 sides?
22. 3 x 9 =
23. 54 ÷ 9 =
24. £5.00 − £3.80 =
25. 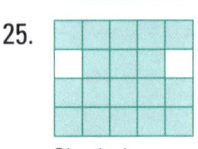 Shaded area = ___ squares

FRIDAY TEST Week 22

1. 36 m − 6 m = ___ m
2. 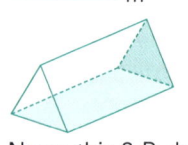 Name this 3-D shape.
3.  Are these two lines parallel?
4. Which fraction is the smallest?
   ☐ $1/2$ ☐ $7/10$
5. 8 x 7 =
6. Difference between 18 and 7.
7. 909p = £
8. Tick the most likely:
   ☐ It will be Saturday tomorrow.
   ☐ You will eat plasticine for tea.
9. Show 9 o'clock on the analogue and digital clocks.
10. Draw a $1/2$ turn anticlockwise. 
11. Tick which contains the most: 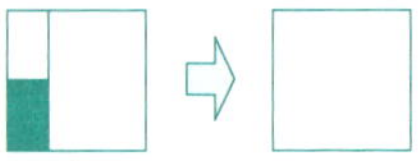
    ☐ 500 mL jug
    ☐ 1 litre jug
12. 400 − ___ = 250
13. What shape is a pizza?
14. How many edges on a cylinder?
15. Which fraction is the largest?
    ☐ $3/4$ ☐ $3/8$
16. Double 50 =
17. Is a circle symmetrical?
18. How many sides on a rectangle?
19. 480 − 120 =
20. Measure the line = ___ cm
21. Round 655 (nearest 100). 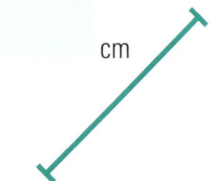
22.  $1/2 = 2/4$ 
    ☐ true ☐ false
23. Difference between 20 and 30.
24. 9, 13, 18, ___, 31
25. 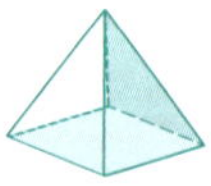 Name this shape.

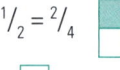

FRIDAY TEST Week 23

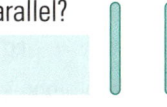

1. 100 m − 75 m = ___ m
2. Round 73 (nearest 10)
3. 600 − ___ = 400
4. 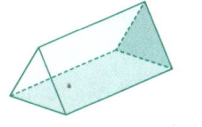 Name this 3-D shape.
5.
   ```
     6 4 5
   + 1 2 3
   ```
6. 0 × 8 =
7. Tick the least likely event.
   ☐ I will turn into a bottle of milk.
   ☐ I will drink some milk.
8. 4 + 8 =
9. 70 − 15 =
10. 500 mL add 250 mL = ___ mL
11. Write these fractions on the number line.
    $\frac{1}{2}$, $\frac{3}{10}$, $\frac{3}{4}$ 
    0 ———————— 1
12. Write six hundred and six as a numeral.
13. 305p = £
14. Are these lines parallel?
15. What is the chance of Sunday following Saturday?
    ☐ impossible
    ☐ possible
    ☐ certain
16.  $\frac{1}{2} = \frac{2}{4}$ 
    ☐ true ☐ false
17. 5 × 3 =
18. Edges on a square pyramid?
19. 81 ÷ 9 =
20. 36 + 24 =
21. Corners on a cube?
22. In 72.3, what is the meaning of the 3?
23. 6, 12, 18, 24,
24. Faces on a triangular pyramid?
25. 330 + 170 =

FRIDAY TEST Week 24

1. 26 cm − 5 cm = ___ cm
2. $3\frac{1}{2}$ m = ___ cm
3. In 28.8 the meaning of the 2 is:
   ☐ 20 ☐ 2 ☐ 0.2
4. Which fraction is the smallest?
   ☐ $\frac{2}{10}$ ☐ $\frac{5}{8}$
5. 3 × 7 =
6. Edges on a square pyramid.
7. 54 ÷ 9 =
8. Write a prime number between 10 and 20.
9. Sum of 4 and 7 =
10. 925p = £
11. Tick the most likely event.
    ☐ You will eat your shoe.
    ☐ You will go to bed tonight.
12.
    ```
      8 5 7
    − 2 4 5
    ```
13. 32 + 38 =
14. Halve 38.
15. 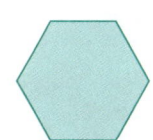 Name this shape.
16. 0.8 > 1
    ☐ true ☐ false
17. 72 − 10 =
18. £10.00 − £3.40 =
19. 49 ÷ 7 =
20. What is the date a week after 25 January?
21. 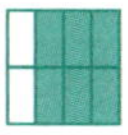 $\frac{6}{8} = \frac{3}{4}$ 
    ☐ true ☐ false
22. Kate has 45p and Sam has 34p. How much altogether? ___ p
23. 8 × 8 =
24. 27 + 4 = 31, so 37 + 4 =
25. 3 + 3 = 2 × 3 =

FRIDAY TEST Week 25

1. 50 cm − 35 cm = ___ cm
2. Circle the parallel lines.

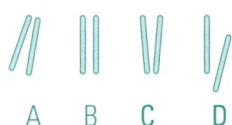

   A   B   C   D
3. 0.2, 0.3, 0.4, ___
4. 8 + 8 + 8 = 3 × 8 = ___
5. What number comes before 600?
6. Can a ◯ tessellate?
7.
   ```
     7 5 4
   − 2 3 1
   ```
8. 35 + 55 =
9. Colour $3/8$
10. Draw a vertical line. 
11. Katie has 35p. John has 42p. How much altogether? ___ p 
12. 6 × 8 =
13. What is $1/2$ of 18?
14. 700 − 440 =
15. Tick the largest.
    ☐ $4/8$ ☐ $8/10$
16. In 672, what is the place value of the 7?
17. What is the chance of you eating peas for dinner?
    ☐ impossible
    ☐ possible
    ☐ certain
18. The date a week before 21 January?
19. How many edges on a cube?
20. Name this shape.
21. Angles in a rectangle?
22. Draw a mirror image (reflection).
23. 5 × 6 = 
24. 24 ÷ 4 =
25. 0.2 > 0.5
    ☐ true ☐ false

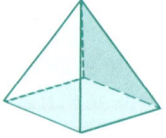

FRIDAY TEST Week 26

1. 12 kg add 8 kg = ___ kg
2. Write eighteen point eight as a numeral.
3. $1/10$ = 0.01 or 0.1?
4. 10 + 10 + 10 = 3 × 10 =
5. What number comes before 700?
6. Washing machines are £500. Fridges are £300. How much altogether?
7. 14 × 0 =
8. What is $1/4$ of 40?
9. How many socks in 8 pairs?
10. 36 + 54 =
11. 5)‾30‾ =
12. Draw as a $3/4$ turn right.
13. Fred has 24 apples. Dana has 13 apples. How many fewer has Dana?
14. Take 6 from 11.
15. 80 ÷ 10 =
16. 21 × 1 =
17. In 39.7, what is the place value of the 7?
18. Tick the smallest
    ☐ $8/10$
    ☐ $1/2$
19. Mark where the right angle is. 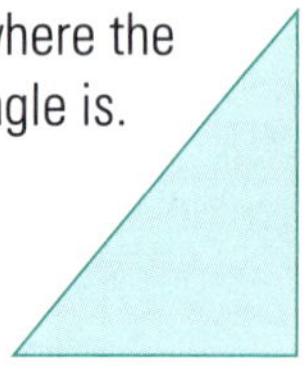
20. How many toes on 4 feet?
21. Using 6, 9 and 3, make the highest possible number.
22. Will a ▢ tessellate?
23. Write as a fraction. 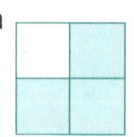
24. Draw a mirror image. 
25. What is the chance of you meeting a dragon on your way home from school?
    ☐ impossible
    ☐ possible
    ☐ not sure
    ☐ might
    ☐ certain

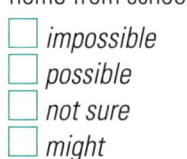

FRIDAY TEST Week 27

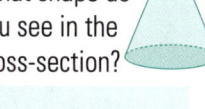

1. 15 kg add 35 kg = ___ kg
2. 7 + 4 =
3. Is W symmetrical?
4. Halve 50 =
5. 230 + 480 =
6. Write five hundred and fifty-five as a numeral.
7. How many eyes on 10 heads? ___ eyes
8. 2 x 3 = 3 x
9. 40 + 40 + 40 + 40 =
10.  Has a square got parallel lines?
11. $6/10$ = 0.6 or 0.06?
12. Kevin has 24 bananas. Angela has 23 bananas. How many altogether?
13. Tick the smallest. ☐ $3/10$ ☐ $5/8$
14. 15 − 9 =
15. The place value of the 4 in 604 is
16. A jumper costs £40 and a pair of trousers £35. How much altogether?
17. Treble 4.
18. 42 x 0 =
19. What shape do you see in the cross-section?
20. 5)‾35 = 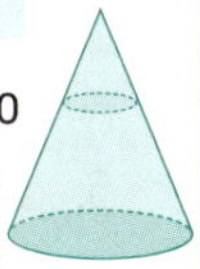
21. Draw a reflection.
22.  Name this shape. 
23. 17 x 1 =
24. What is $3/4$ of 20? =
25. Shaded area = ___ squares

FRIDAY TEST Week 28

1. 48 kg − 18 kg = ___ kg
2. $8/10$ = 0.
3. 14 − 9 =
4. If you rode 5 km in a quarter of an hour, how far could you ride in 1 hour? ___ km
5. 24 x 0 =
6. 15 + 5 =
7. Treble 7 =
8. 3 x 4 = 4 x
9. 8)‾32 =
10. Has a rectangle got parallel sides?
11. How many gloves in 8 pairs? 
12. What is $5/10$ of 20?
13. Judy has 64p. Kara has 22p. How much more has Judy? ___ p
14.  Name this shape.
15. Round 859 (nearest 100).
16. Tick the smallest. ☐ $3/4$ ☐ $2/8$
17. 29 x 1 =
18. Double 37.
19. 6 x 4 = 24 = 8 x
20. Will this  tessellate?
21. Is A or B vertical?
22. How many days in 3 full weeks? 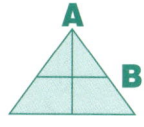
23. 8 + 3 + 3 =
24. $6/8$ = $3/4$ ☐ true ☐ false
25. Write the fractions on the number line. $2/8$, $3/4$, $6/10$

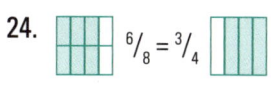

FRIDAY TEST Week 29

1. 79 kg − 19 kg = ___ kg
2. 40 − 9 =
3. 40 + 80 =
4. The date a week after 27 March is ___.
5. 7)‾28 =
6. 18 × 10 =
7. 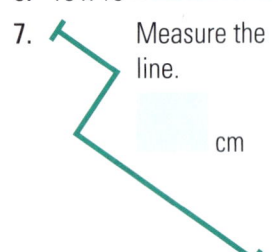 Measure the line. ___ cm
8. $\frac{4}{8}$ of 20 =
9. Has a triangle got parallel lines?
10. How many right angles in a rectangle?
11. 45 + 35 =
12. Mary has 79p. Kate has 54p. How much more has Mary? ___ p
13. Draw a $\frac{3}{4}$ turn right. 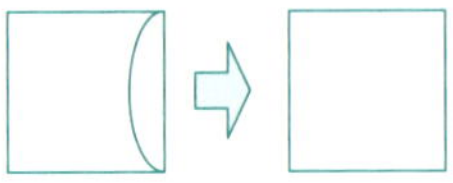
14. £5.30 + £3.70 =
15. Write a symmetrical numeral.
16. Is a cube 2-D or 3-D?
17. Share 36 sweets between 6 children. How many each?
18. If you walked 4 km in 30 minutes, how far would you walk in an hour? ___ km
19. 8 × 3 = 3 × ___
20. 93, 89, 85, 81, ___
21. 23 × 2 =
22. How many edges on a triangular prism? 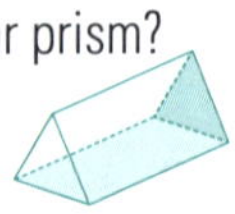
23. 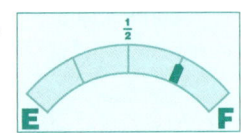 How much fuel has been used? ☐ $\frac{1}{4}$ ☐ $\frac{1}{2}$ ☐ $\frac{3}{4}$
24. Write eighty-three point five as a numeral.
25. 9 × 8 =

FRIDAY TEST Week 30

1. 300 g + 350 g = ___ g
2. 14 − 4 =
3. 7 × 5 = 5 × ___
4. 300 + 200 + 100 =
5. 21 × 10 =
6. 7)‾42 =
7. What two shapes make a cylinder?
8. Share 35 nuts between 5 squirrels. How many each?
9. Has a square got parallel lines? 
10. 1.8, 1.4, ___, 0.6, 0.2
11. 0.3 > 0.5 ☐ true ☐ false
12. Edges on a cone?
13. £1.00 − 45p =
14. What is $\frac{1}{2}$ of 48?
15. 12 × 3 =
16. 600 − 210 =
17. Ben has 99 marbles. Mandy has 74. How many fewer has Mandy?
18. Draw a reflection. 
19. Judy has 32 cakes. She sells 24. How many has she got left?
20. 7 × 8 =
21. What is a $\frac{1}{4}$ of 8?
22. Draw parallel lines.
23. Treble 8 =
24. What month on 21.8.06?
25. Can a rectangle tessellate?

FRIDAY TEST Week 31

1. 240 g – 30 g = ____ g
2. 3 x 6 =
3. 15 – 9 =
4. Cost of 5 m of rope at 10p per 10 cm = £
5. In 34.5, what is the place value of the 3?
6. 9 ÷ 2 = ____ r
7. 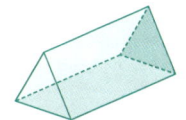 Name this 3-D shape.
8. 6 x 4 = (2 x 4) + (____ x 4)
9. 1 4 x 2
10. $\frac{1}{10}$ = 0.5 ☐ true ☐ false
11. 280 + 120 =
12. 3 x 8 =
13. 4)‾24 =
14. 500 mL add 250 mL = ____ mL
15. £2.99 = ____ p
16. Will a cube roll?
17. Tick the right angle.
18. 0 + 7 = 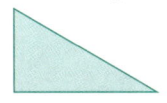
19. Surfaces on a solid cylinder.
20. What is the chance of it snowing today?
    ☐ impossible
    ☐ not sure
    ☐ possible
    ☐ might
    ☐ certain
21.  $\frac{1}{4} = \frac{4}{8}$ ☐ true ☐ false
22. £3.00 – £1.10 =
23. Tick the largest. ☐ 0.1 ☐ 0.9 ☐ 0.3
24. Write the fractions on the number line. $\frac{1}{4}, \frac{9}{10}, \frac{4}{8}$
25. Draw a line of symmetry. 

FRIDAY TEST Week 32

1. 50 kg add 75 kg = ____ kg
2. Draw a reflection.
3. 8 ÷ 3 = ____ r 
4. 7 x 4 =
5. 27 + 10 =
6. Write nine hundred and ninety-nine as a numeral.
7. 9 x 5 = (5 x 5) + (____ x 5)
8. Does a cube have right angles?
9. 1 2 x 4
10.  This shape has been turned $\frac{1}{4}$
    ☐ clockwise.
    ☐ anticlockwise.
11. 45 ÷ 7 = ____ r
12. 240 + 30 =
13. 100, 95, 90, 85, 80, ____
14.  Name this shape.
15. £2.55 – 60p =
16. Can this 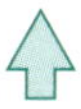 tessellate?
17. Circle the largest. 0.4 0.7 0.3
18. $\frac{3}{10}$ = 0.3 ☐ true ☐ false
19. 15 litres + 25 litres = ____ litres
20. Write the fractions on the number line. $\frac{1}{2}, \frac{6}{8}, \frac{2}{10}$
21. 13 – 9 = 
22. £7.05 = ____ p
23. 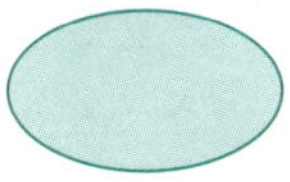 Name this shape.
24. 15 – 10 =
25. Cost of buying 1 kg of tomatoes at 10p per 100 g = £

FRIDAY TEST Week 33

1. 20 minutes to 4. 
2. 3 + 3 + 3 + 3 =
3. 9 + 7 =
4. 9 ÷ 4 =   r
5. Does a cuboid have right angles?
6. Draw a vertical line.
7. 5 x 7 =
   (2 x 5) + (x 5)
8.   2 3
   x   2
9. $5/10$ = 0.5
   ☐ true ☐ false
10. Write seven hundred and one as a numeral.
11. 15 litres subtract 11 litres =
       litres
12. £8.50 =   p
13. Write the fractions on the number line.
    $3/4$, $2/8$, $6/10$ 
    0 ——————— 1
14. How many triangles can you find? 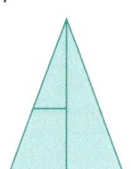
15. What shape is a tin of dog food?
16. 52 – 10 =
17. Difference between 10 and 5.
18. Is Z symmetrical?
19. Halve 96.
20. Name this 3-D shape.
21. Circle the largest.
    0.4   0.6   0.1
22. £5.20 + £4.80 =
23. Can a cuboid stack?
24. 9 x 5 =
25. Share 36 bones between 6 hungry dogs. How many each?

FRIDAY TEST Week 34

1. 3.55 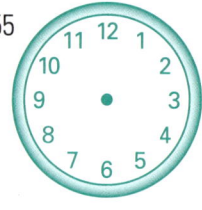
2. 5)‾27 =   r
3. Write one point five as a numeral.
4. Round 294 (nearest 10).
5. 8 x 3 =
   (3 x 3) + (x 3)
6. 50 + 90 =
7. Write from smallest to largest.
   0.9   0.3   0.4
8. 4 x 3 = 12, so 12 ÷ 3 =
9.   2 3
   x   2
10. 25 cm add 50 cm =
       cm

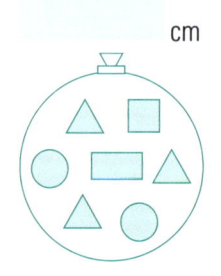

The chance of choosing the following shapes from the bag is:

11. Circle =   in 7.
12. Square = 1 in   .
13. Triangle =   in   .

14. Cost of 6 kg of chocolate at £2.00 per 500 g?
    £
15. How many angles in a hexagon?
16. Difference between 11 and 3.
17. 0.5 = $5/10$
    ☐ true ☐ false
18. 400 + 500 =
19. Name this shape.
20. 405p =
    £
21. Is this angle more or less than a right angle? 
22. A 6-sided shape is a   .
23. 8 x 7 =
24. Number of faces in a cube?
25. Which 2 shapes are the faces of a triangular prism?
       and

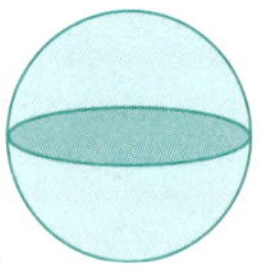

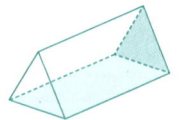

FRIDAY TEST Week 35

1. 2:20 ___ past ___
2. 6)21 = ___ r ___
3. 130 − 60 =
4. Is this angle more or less than a right angle?
5. What shape is this?
6. 72, 63, 54, 45, ___
7. Is 2/4 equivalent to 5/10?
8. 3 4 x 2
9. 7 x 3 = 21, so 21 ÷ 7 =
10. How many triangles can you find?
11. If you rode your bike 9 km in half an hour, how far would you ride in an hour? ___ km
12. Write from smallest to largest. 0.3 0.5 0.2
13. Colour 3/4 of the pears.
14. 60 cm − 35 cm = ___ cm
15. 305p = £
16. Share 27 sweets between 9 children. How many each?
17. 6 x 4 =
18. Write the decimals on the number line. 0.7 0.2 0.6
19. 0.9 = 8/10 ☐ true ☐ false
20. How many gloves in 9 pairs?
21. 9 x 2 =
22. £10.00 − £2.60 =
23. Tick the most likely event:
    ☐ The weather will be wet this evening.
    ☐ The weather will be dry this evening.
24. 8 x 6 =
25. Draw parallel lines.

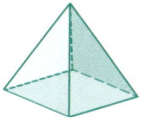

FRIDAY TEST Week 36

1. 8:50 ___ to ___
2. Sum of 90 and 40 =
3. Write from smallest to largest. 0.7 0.2 0.9
4. Write seven hundred and two as a numeral.
5. 165p = £
6. 10)35 = ___ r
7. 3 3 x 2
8. 1/4 of 28 =
9. 300 + 70 + 6 =
10. 6 x 3 = 18, so 18 ÷ 6 =
11. 75 m add 25 m = ___ m
12. What is the difference between 18 and 8?
13. Is this 5 symmetrical?
14. 0.4 = 4/10 ☐ true ☐ false
15. 3 ÷ 3 =
16. If the date is 28 October, what will the date be in 4 days?
17. 6 x 9 =
18. Is this angle more or less than a right angle?
19. Draw a reflection.
20. £4.00 + £1.25 =
21. How many eyes on 8 faces?
22. 9 x 0 =
23. 2)17 = ___ r
24. Tick which lines the above shape has.
    ☐ parallel
    ☐ vertical
    ☐ horizontal
25. Tick the least likely event:
    ☐ The grass will become pink next week.
    ☐ The grass will still be green next week.

FRIDAY TEST Week 37

1. Ten to 8.
   [:]
2. 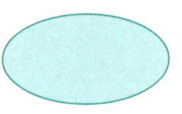 [oval shape] Name this shape.
3. 3 × 8 =
4. 80 + 70 =
5. 42 × 2
6. 60 + 70 =
7. In 478, which number represents the lowest value?
8. $2/10$ = 0.5
   ☐ true ☐ false
9. 4.6 m = ___ cm
10. 900 – 780 =
11. $3/4$ of 16 =
12. Tick which lines a cube has. 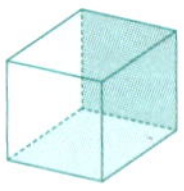
    ☐ parallel
    ☐ vertical
    ☐ horizontal
13. 8)26 = ___ r
14. 500 + 300 =
15. Is a lolly stick symmetrical?
16. $1/2$ of a number is 14. What is the number?
17. 100 m – 75 m = ___ m
18. 7 × 8 = 56, so 56 ÷ 7 =
19. Draw a horizontal line.
20. 180 – 90 =
21. Halve 72.
22. Is this angle more or less than a right angle? 
23. 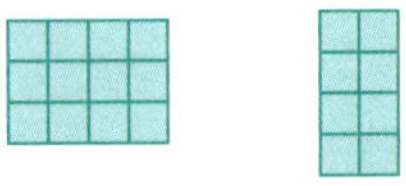 A   B
    Which shape has a larger area?
24. Is $2/4$ equivalent to $4/8$?
25. Surfaces on a solid cylinder?

FRIDAY TEST Week 38

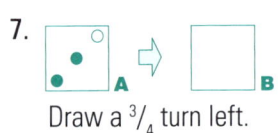

1. Twenty-five past 3.
   [:]
2. Using all the numerals, arrange them into the largest number.
   4 7 0
3. $5/10$ = 0.2
   ☐ true ☐ false
4. Write from largest to smallest.
   0.3   0.8   0.4
5. 16 + 8 =
6. Edges on a sphere?
7. [square with dots → square] A   B
   Draw a $3/4$ turn left.
8. 400 + 500 =
9. Which is longer?
   ☐ 1 m ☐ 10 cm

The chance of pulling the following coloured beads from the bag is:
[bag with beads: r, g, r, b, y, y, g, g, r, g]

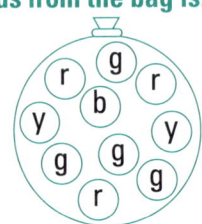

10. red = ___ in
11. green = ___ in
12. yellow = ___ in
13. blue = ___ in
14. Draw an oval.
15. $1/4$ of a number is 6. What is the number?
16. 14 – 6 =
17. 9 × 3 =
18. 12 × 8 = 96
    ☐ true ☐ false
19. 23 × 3
20. 140 – 90 =
21. 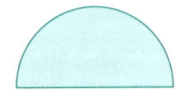 [semicircle] Name this shape.
22. Round 195 (nearest ten).
23. Angles in a hexagon?
24. 6)38 = ___ r
25. Draw a reflection.
    4|

FRIDAY TEST Week 39

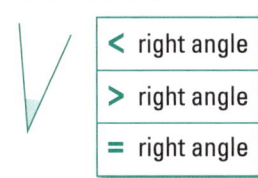

1. $1\frac{1}{2}$ hours =
   ___ hour(s)
   ___ minute(s)
2. David has 79p. Steven has 55p. How much more has David?
   ___ p
3. 90 + 90 + 90 =
4. How many toes on 6 feet?
5. Draw an arrow showing anticlockwise.
6. 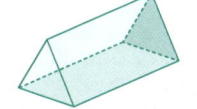 Name this shape.
7. 900 − ___ = 450
8. Write from smallest to largest.
   0.6   0.3   0.9
9. 6 × 5 =
10. Tick the analogue clock.
    (a) ☐ 
    (b) ☐ 9:00
11. Share 30 sweets between 6 children. How many each?
12. 0, 3, 6, 9
    Rule =
13. Write the decimals on the number line.
    0.7   0.2   0.4 
    0 ——————— 1
14. Circle the answer
    < right angle
    > right angle
    = right angle
15. 4 1
    × 2
16. Double 38.
17. 3 × 8 = 24,
    24 ÷ 3 =
    8 × 3 =
    24 ÷ 8 =
18. 4)27 = ___ r
19. 250 + 550 =
20. 6 × 8 =
21.  Draw a $\frac{1}{4}$ turn left.
22. $\frac{3}{4}$ of a number is 27. What is the number?
23. 0.3 = $\frac{3}{10}$
    ☐ true ☐ false
24. 14 + 17 =
25. Draw a reflection.

FRIDAY TEST Week 40

1.  ___ past
2. 3 2
    × 3
3. 9 × 10 =
4. $\frac{1}{10}$ of a number is 8. What is the number?
5. £0.80 + £0.70 =
6. Katy has 86p. John has 34p. How much more has Katy?
   ___ p
7. Tick which lines this shape has:
   ☐ parallel
   ☐ vertical
   ☐ horizontal 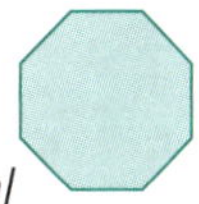
8. $\frac{7}{10}$ = 0.1
   ☐ true ☐ false
9. 6 × 5 =
10. Draw a reflection. 
11. 4)33 = ___ r
12. 700 − 440 =
13. Circle the answer. 
    < right angle
    > right angle
    = right angle
14. 20 − 4 =
15. 4 + 6 + 4 =
16. 6 × 3 = 18,
    18 ÷ 3 =
    3 × 6 =
    18 ÷ 6 =
17. 9 + 2 =
18. Write from largest to smallest.
    0.2   0.7   0.4
19. £1.00 − 55p =
20. 7 × 6 =
21. Should a flag pole be vertical or horizontal?
22.  Name this shape. 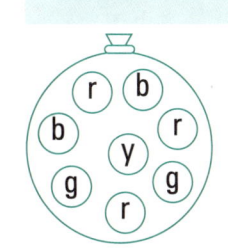
23. Which colour has the greatest chance of being picked?
24. Which colour has the least chance of being picked?
25. Which two colours share an equal chance of being picked?

MATHS FACTS

Place value

741.2
700.0
 40.0
  1.0
   .2

hundreds	tens	units	•	tenths
7	4	1	·	2

Addition and subtraction facts

This table will remind you of the addition and subtraction facts to 20.

+	0	1	2	3	4	5	6	7	8	9	10
0	0	1	2	3	4	5	6	7	8	9	10
1	1	2	3	4	5	6	7	8	9	10	11
2	2	3	4	5	6	7	8	9	10	11	12
3	3	4	5	6	7	8	9	10	11	12	13
4	4	5	6	7	8	9	10	11	12	13	14
5	5	6	7	8	9	10	11	12	13	14	15
6	6	7	8	9	10	11	12	13	14	15	16
7	7	8	9	10	11	12	13	14	15	16	17
8	8	9	10	11	12	13	14	15	16	17	18
9	9	10	11	12	13	14	15	16	17	18	19
10	10	11	12	13	14	15	16	17	18	19	20

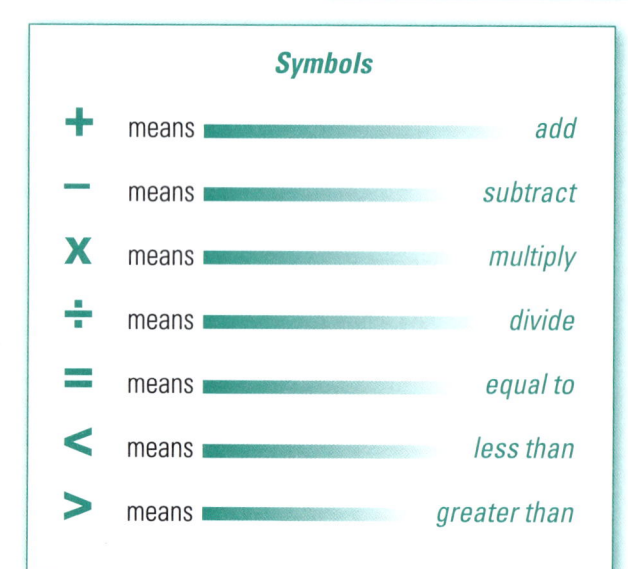

Symbols

+ means add
− means subtract
× means multiply
÷ means divide
= means equal to
< means less than
> means greater than

Odd and even numbers

Odd numbers end in 1, 3, 5, 7 or 9.
For example: 54, 317, 821, 999

Even numbers end in 0, 2, 4, 6 or 8.
For example: 54, 720, 636, 998

New wave mental maths

MATHS FACTS

Multiplication and division facts

Multiplication and division facts are linked together. If you know one multiplication fact you also have the ability to know three other related facts.

For example:
If you know the fact   4 x 5 = 20
You will also know the facts   5 x 4 = 20 and 20 ÷ 4 = 5 and 20 ÷ 5 = 4

2x

table	other facts I know		
1 x 2 = 2	2 x 1 = 2	2 ÷ 2 = 1	2 ÷ 1 = 2
2 x 2 = 4		4 ÷ 2 = 2	
3 x 2 = 6	2 x 3 = 6	6 ÷ 2 = 3	6 ÷ 3 = 2
4 x 2 = 8	2 x 4 = 8	8 ÷ 2 = 4	8 ÷ 4 = 2
5 x 2 = 10	2 x 5 = 10	10 ÷ 2 = 5	10 ÷ 5 = 2
6 x 2 = 12	2 x 6 = 12	12 ÷ 2 = 6	12 ÷ 6 = 2
7 x 2 = 14	2 x 7 = 14	14 ÷ 2 = 7	14 ÷ 7 = 2
8 x 2 = 16	2 x 8 = 16	16 ÷ 2 = 8	16 ÷ 8 = 2
9 x 2 = 18	2 x 9 = 18	18 ÷ 2 = 9	18 ÷ 9 = 2
10 x 2 = 20	2 x 10 = 20	20 ÷ 2 = 10	20 ÷ 10 = 2

3x

table	other facts I know		
1 x 3 = 3	3 x 1 = 3	3 ÷ 3 = 1	3 ÷ 1 = 3
2 x 3 = 6	3 x 2 = 6	6 ÷ 3 = 2	6 ÷ 2 = 3
3 x 3 = 9		9 ÷ 3 = 3	
4 x 3 = 12	3 x 4 = 12	12 ÷ 3 = 4	12 ÷ 4 = 3
5 x 3 = 15	3 x 5 = 15	15 ÷ 3 = 5	15 ÷ 5 = 3
6 x 3 = 18	3 x 6 = 18	18 ÷ 3 = 6	18 ÷ 6 = 3
7 x 3 = 21	3 x 7 = 21	21 ÷ 3 = 7	21 ÷ 7 = 3
8 x 3 = 24	3 x 8 = 24	24 ÷ 3 = 8	24 ÷ 8 = 3
9 x 3 = 27	3 x 9 = 27	27 ÷ 3 = 9	27 ÷ 9 = 3
10 x 3 = 30	3 x 10 = 30	30 ÷ 3 = 10	30 ÷ 10 = 3

4x

table	other facts I know		
1 x 4 = 4	4 x 1 = 4	4 ÷ 4 = 1	4 ÷ 1 = 4
2 x 4 = 8	4 x 2 = 8	8 ÷ 4 = 2	8 ÷ 2 = 4
3 x 4 = 12	4 x 3 = 12	12 ÷ 4 = 3	12 ÷ 3 = 4
4 x 4 = 16		16 ÷ 4 = 4	
5 x 4 = 20	4 x 5 = 20	20 ÷ 4 = 5	20 ÷ 5 = 4
6 x 4 = 24	4 x 6 = 24	24 ÷ 4 = 6	24 ÷ 6 = 4
7 x 4 = 28	4 x 7 = 28	28 ÷ 4 = 7	28 ÷ 7 = 4
8 x 4 = 32	4 x 8 = 32	32 ÷ 4 = 8	32 ÷ 8 = 4
9 x 4 = 36	4 x 9 = 36	36 ÷ 4 = 9	36 ÷ 9 = 4
10 x 4 = 40	4 x 10 = 40	40 ÷ 4 = 10	40 ÷ 10 = 4

5x

table	other facts I know		
1 x 5 = 5	5 x 1 = 5	5 ÷ 5 = 1	5 ÷ 1 = 5
2 x 5 = 10	5 x 2 = 10	10 ÷ 5 = 2	10 ÷ 2 = 5
3 x 5 = 15	5 x 3 = 15	15 ÷ 5 = 3	15 ÷ 3 = 5
4 x 5 = 20	5 x 4 = 20	20 ÷ 5 = 4	20 ÷ 4 = 5
5 x 5 = 25		25 ÷ 5 = 5	
6 x 5 = 30	5 x 6 = 30	30 ÷ 5 = 6	30 ÷ 6 = 5
7 x 5 = 35	5 x 7 = 35	35 ÷ 5 = 7	35 ÷ 7 = 5
8 x 5 = 40	5 x 8 = 40	40 ÷ 5 = 8	40 ÷ 8 = 5
9 x 5 = 45	5 x 9 = 45	45 ÷ 5 = 9	45 ÷ 9 = 5
10 x 5 = 50	5 x 10 = 50	50 ÷ 5 = 10	50 ÷ 10 = 5

6x

table	other facts I know		
1 x 6 = 6	6 x 1 = 6	6 ÷ 6 = 1	6 ÷ 1 = 6
2 x 6 = 12	6 x 2 = 12	12 ÷ 6 = 2	12 ÷ 2 = 6
3 x 6 = 18	6 x 3 = 18	18 ÷ 6 = 3	18 ÷ 3 = 6
4 x 6 = 24	6 x 4 = 24	24 ÷ 6 = 4	24 ÷ 4 = 6
5 x 6 = 30	6 x 5 = 30	30 ÷ 6 = 5	30 ÷ 5 = 6
6 x 6 = 36		36 ÷ 6 = 6	
7 x 6 = 42	6 x 7 = 42	42 ÷ 6 = 7	42 ÷ 7 = 6
8 x 6 = 48	6 x 8 = 48	48 ÷ 6 = 8	48 ÷ 8 = 6
9 x 6 = 54	6 x 9 = 54	54 ÷ 6 = 9	54 ÷ 9 = 6
10 x 6 = 60	6 x 10 = 60	60 ÷ 6 = 10	60 ÷ 10 = 6

7x

table	other facts I know		
1 x 7 = 7	7 x 1 = 7	7 ÷ 7 = 1	7 ÷ 1 = 7
2 x 7 = 14	7 x 2 = 14	14 ÷ 7 = 2	14 ÷ 2 = 7
3 x 7 = 21	7 x 3 = 21	21 ÷ 7 = 3	21 ÷ 3 = 7
4 x 7 = 28	7 x 4 = 28	28 ÷ 7 = 4	28 ÷ 4 = 7
5 x 7 = 35	7 x 5 = 35	35 ÷ 7 = 5	35 ÷ 5 = 7
6 x 7 = 42	7 x 6 = 42	42 ÷ 7 = 6	42 ÷ 6 = 7
7 x 7 = 49		49 ÷ 7 = 7	
8 x 7 = 56	7 x 8 = 56	56 ÷ 7 = 8	56 ÷ 8 = 7
9 x 7 = 63	7 x 9 = 63	63 ÷ 7 = 9	63 ÷ 9 = 7
10 x 7 = 70	7 x 10 = 70	70 ÷ 7 = 10	70 ÷ 10 = 7

MATHS FACTS

8x

table	other facts I know		
1 x 8 = 8	8 x 1 = 8	8 ÷ 8 = 1	8 ÷ 1 = 8
2 x 8 = 16	8 x 2 = 16	16 ÷ 8 = 2	16 ÷ 2 = 8
3 x 8 = 24	8 x 3 = 24	24 ÷ 8 = 3	24 ÷ 3 = 8
4 x 8 = 32	8 x 4 = 32	32 ÷ 8 = 4	32 ÷ 4 = 8
5 x 8 = 40	8 x 5 = 40	40 ÷ 8 = 5	40 ÷ 5 = 8
6 x 8 = 48	8 x 6 = 48	48 ÷ 8 = 6	48 ÷ 6 = 8
7 x 8 = 56	8 x 7 = 56	56 ÷ 8 = 7	56 ÷ 7 = 8
8 x 8 = 64		64 ÷ 8 = 8	
9 x 8 = 72	8 x 9 = 72	72 ÷ 8 = 9	72 ÷ 9 = 8
10 x 8 = 80	8 x 10 = 80	80 ÷ 8 = 10	80 ÷ 10 = 8

9x

table	other facts I know		
1 x 9 = 9	9 x 1 = 9	9 ÷ 9 = 1	9 ÷ 1 = 9
2 x 9 = 18	9 x 2 = 18	18 ÷ 9 = 2	18 ÷ 2 = 9
3 x 9 = 27	9 x 3 = 27	27 ÷ 9 = 3	27 ÷ 3 = 9
4 x 9 = 36	9 x 4 = 36	36 ÷ 9 = 4	36 ÷ 4 = 9
5 x 9 = 45	9 x 5 = 45	45 ÷ 9 = 5	45 ÷ 5 = 9
6 x 9 = 54	9 x 6 = 54	54 ÷ 9 = 6	54 ÷ 6 = 9
7 x 9 = 63	9 x 7 = 63	63 ÷ 9 = 7	63 ÷ 7 = 9
8 x 9 = 72	9 x 8 = 72	72 ÷ 9 = 8	72 ÷ 8 = 9
9 x 9 = 81		81 ÷ 9 = 9	
10 x 9 = 90	9 x 10 = 90	90 ÷ 9 = 10	90 ÷ 10 = 9

10x

table	other facts I know		
1 x 10 = 10	10 x 1 = 10	10 ÷ 10 = 1	10 ÷ 1 = 10
2 x 10 = 20	10 x 2 = 20	20 ÷ 10 = 2	20 ÷ 2 = 10
3 x 10 = 30	10 x 3 = 30	30 ÷ 10 = 3	30 ÷ 3 = 10
4 x 10 = 40	10 x 4 = 40	40 ÷ 10 = 4	40 ÷ 4 = 10
5 x 10 = 50	10 x 5 = 50	50 ÷ 10 = 5	50 ÷ 5 = 10
6 x 10 = 60	10 x 6 = 60	60 ÷ 10 = 6	60 ÷ 6 = 10
7 x 10 = 70	10 x 7 = 70	70 ÷ 10 = 7	70 ÷ 7 = 10
8 x 10 = 80	10 x 8 = 80	80 ÷ 10 = 8	80 ÷ 8 = 10
9 x 10 = 90	10 x 9 = 90	90 ÷ 10 = 9	90 ÷ 9 = 10
10 x 10 = 100		100 ÷ 10 = 10	

Fractions

Numerator — The number above the line, indicating how many parts are in consideration.

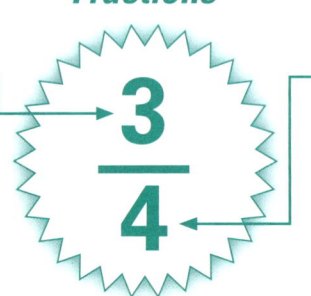

$\frac{3}{4}$

Denominator — The number below the line, indicating how many parts the whole number is divided into.

Equivalent fractions

one whole										
½						½				
¼			¼			¼			¼		
⅛	⅛	⅛	⅛	⅛	⅛	⅛	⅛		
1/10	1/10	1/10	1/10	1/10	1/10	1/10	1/10	1/10	1/10

MATHS FACTS

Fractions

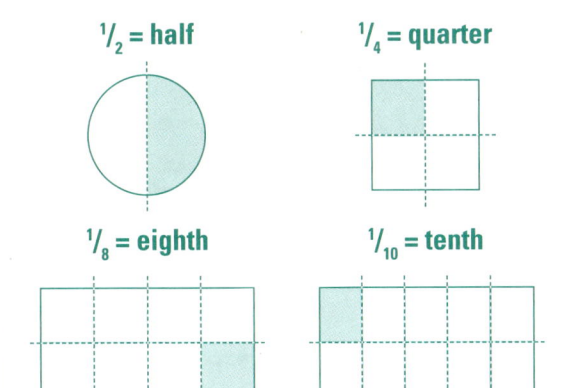

$1/2$ = half
$1/4$ = quarter
$1/8$ = eighth
$1/10$ = tenth

Fractions and decimals

Fraction	Decimal
$1/2$	0.5
$1/4$	0.25
$1/8$	0.125
$1/10$	0.1

2-D shapes

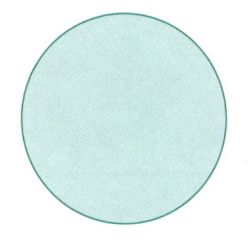

circle
1 side
0 corners

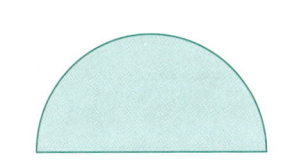

semicircle
2 sides
2 corners

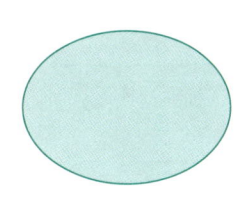

oval
1 side
0 corners

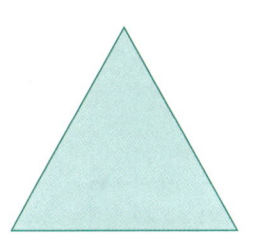

triangle
3 sides
3 corners

square
4 sides
4 corners

rectangle
4 sides
4 corners

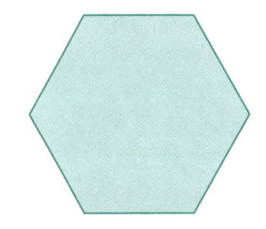

hexagon
6 sides
6 corners

3-D shapes

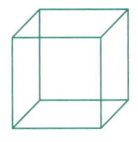

cube
6 faces
12 edges
8 vertices

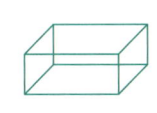

cuboid
6 faces
12 edges
8 vertices

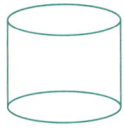

cylinder
3 surfaces
0 edges
0 vertices

cone
2 surfaces
0 edges
1 vertex

sphere
1 surface
0 edges
0 vertices

triangular prism
5 faces
9 edges
6 vertices

pyramid
5 faces
8 edges
5 vertices

Prim-Ed Publishing   www.prim-ed.com   New wave mental maths

MATHS FACTS

Nets of 3-D shapes

cube

cone

cuboid

triangular prism

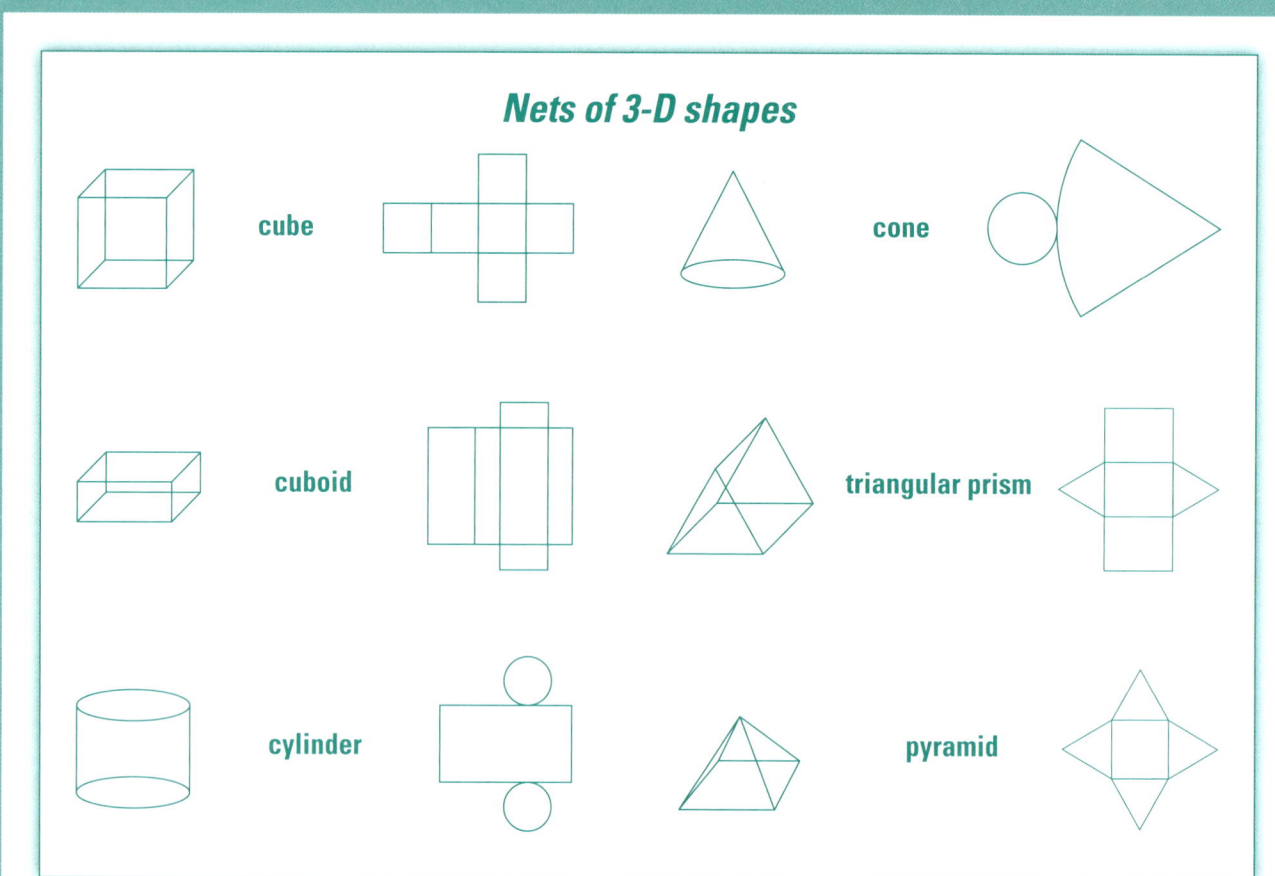

cylinder

pyramid

Lines

Horizontal
A line parallel to the horizon.

Vertical
A line which is at right angles to a horizontal line.

Parallel
Lines that are always the same distance apart and have no common points.

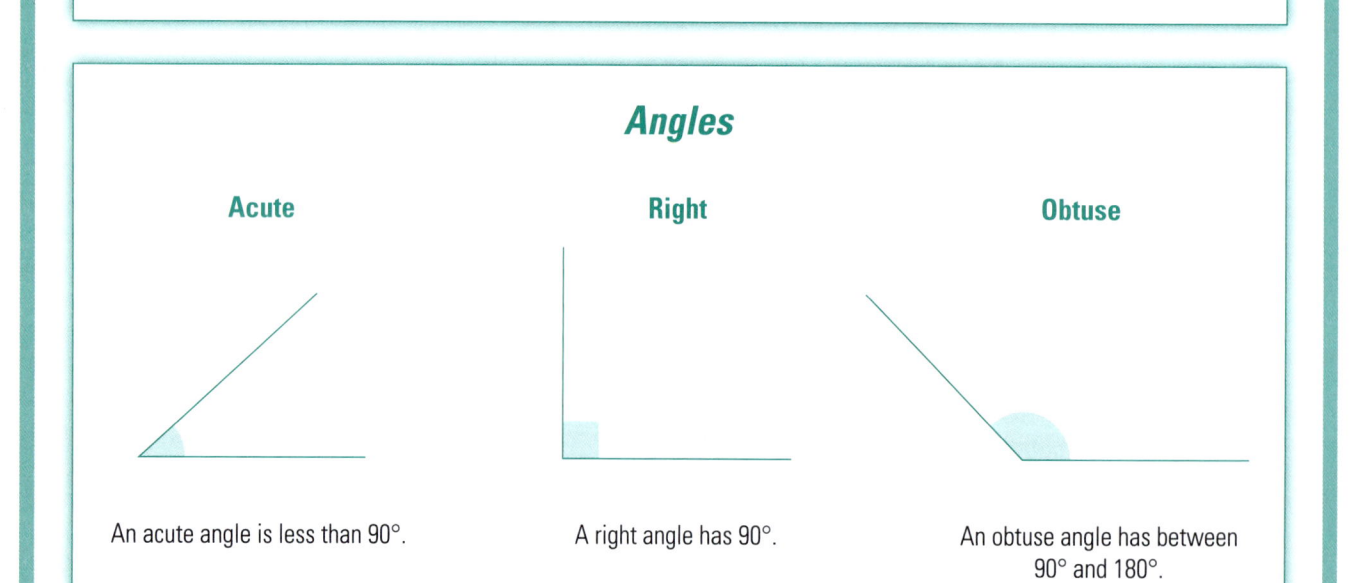

Angles

Acute

Right

Obtuse

An acute angle is less than 90°.

A right angle has 90°.

An obtuse angle has between 90° and 180°.

MATHS FACTS

Length

Unit	Abbreviation
centimetre	cm
metre	m

100 cm = 1 m

Weight

Unit	Abbreviation
gram	g
kilogram	kg

1000 g = 1 kg

Capacity

Unit	Abbreviation
millilitre	mL
litre	L

1000 mL = 1 L

Money

Unit	Symbol
pence	p
pound	£

100p = £1.00

Money

1p one pence

5p five pence

20p twenty pence

£1 one pound

2p two pence

10p ten pence

50p fifty pence

£2 two pounds

MATHS FACTS

Time

Analogue	Digital
(clock showing 7:15)	*7:15*
(clock showing 1:50)	*1:50*

60 seconds = 1 minute

60 minutes = 1 hour

24 hours = 1 day

7 days = 1 week

52 weeks = 1 year

Pictograms

A graph in which data is represented by pictures. One picture could represent one unit or many.

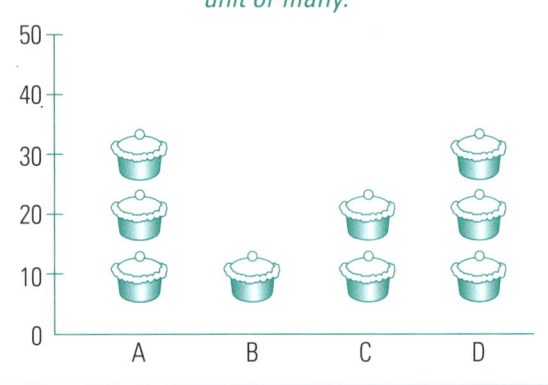

Bar graphs

A graph which represents information regarding frequency of outcomes using bar lengths.

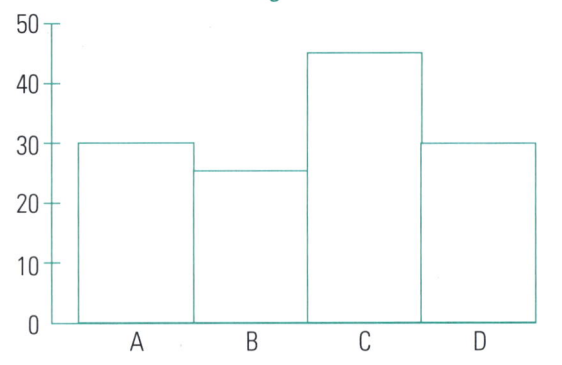

Chance

The likelihood of an event occurring.

For example:

A baby has a 1 in 2 chance of being born a girl.

This is written 1 : 2

We have a 1 in 6 chance of throwing a 6 on a die.

This is written 1 : 6